When the Guyanian Tragedy ~~~~~
— The Big Question Was

# WHY?

## PEOPLE'S TEMPLE
## PEOPLE'S TOMB

"I have Mafia connections, and they will stand with me all the way" - Jim Jones

"My father was a very frightened man" - Stephan Jones

"Jones ties to Russia and Cuba hinted cult leader reportedly planned to form own jungle state" - *Los Angeles Times*

"Shows the difference between true Christianity and the cults" - *The Courier-News*

"Jones ceased to preach Christianity and began to preach that he himself was Christ" - *Seattle Times*

"Chief of cult, double con-man" - *Oregon Journal*

# POSSESSED BY PARANOIA...

It has been said that the love of power is the most fundamental of all human motives. Driven by an insatiable desire to control his followers, Jim Jones tormented, twisted, and taunted his "family" until they submitted their wills, their bodies, their minds and spirits to his brutal tyranny.

No novelist could conceive a more demented plot or devise a story so gruesome and strange. This is the grim and shocking account of Jonestown—and why it happened. Here is Jim Jones from a new perspective, with insights into how and why this former choirboy and ordained minister has found his place in history's gallery of madmen. More importantly, it is the story of a follower who questioned—and found the truth.

Under the People's Temple pavilion in Guyana there is a fitting epitaph for the victims of Jim Jones's brand of religion. It says simply, "Those who do not remember the past are condemned to repeat it." This book was written with that thought in mind—so that the world would remember Jonestown and, through greater understanding, never permit a repetition of its atrocities.

# PEOPLE'S TEMPLE
# TEMPLE
## PEOPLE'S TOMB

# PEOPLE'S TEMPLE
# PEOPLE'S TOMB

## BY PHIL KERNS with Doug Wead

Logos International
Plainfield, New Jersey

Special thanks

to Peggy Soric of the
Springfield Leader Express

Russ Chandler of the
Los Angeles Times

Donnis Battey, Louanna Wasson
and Susan Wimmer

*The authors are donating their royalties to provide ways for those who have been involved in cults to receive spiritual help.*

*Dedicated to*
*my mother and sister Carol,*
*who lost their lives*
*while in search of a dream*
*in Guyana.*

# *Acknowledgment*

My special thanks to Rev. Ross Case who freely shared his research material related to this story. Attracted to Jim Jones in the early days of People's Temple, Rev. Case eventually left the cult to devote his time to exposing Jones's departure from true Christianity, trying to warn cult members of imminent dangers.

Special thanks also to Dennis Roberts.

# Contents

# one

# "There's Going To Be a Mass Suicide!"

On Saturday evening, November 18, 1978, my wife and I were watching the NBC special "Heroes of the Bible." Suddenly the program was interrupted. "We have an NBC news bulletin. There is an unconfirmed report of a shooting incident in Guyana, South America. The report states that unknown persons fired on California Congressman Leo Ryan and members of his party as they attempted to board their aircraft at the Port Kaituma Airstrip. It is believed that NBC reporter Don Harris was killed. Congressman Ryan was visiting Guyana to investigate a California religious cult which had established a commune there. NBC will keep you advised of any further developments in the story."

1

I jumped from my chair and grabbed my head, "O dear Jesus. O God, you've got to do something. Now!"

My wife, Vicki, stayed glued to the television as if another news report would come back on. "Calm down," she said. "Calm down."

"My sister and my mother are down there," I shouted back. "The suicide pact! Remember? The suicide pact. I've got to get down there. Get my clothes together."

"Stop it! Stop it!" she screamed. The suicide pact. It was all so preposterous. I had told her before but to what extent she believed me I never knew. I rushed into the bedroom throwing clothes madly into a suitcase. "Where are you going?" she asked, following me back to the door.

"To the Portland airport," I snapped. "I've got to get to South America before they kill themselves."

"Wait! Phil, honey, please. Wait! Call someone first." Vicki pleaded with me and then to stall for time she said, "Make a reservation. Maybe you won't get on."

We have an office in our home. I went in, sat down, massaged my head and tried to think. Calm down. Vicki's first words seemed to just reach my conscious level. All right, calm, calm, easy does it. You have a pretty wild story. At best nobody will believe you but if you sound too excited you'll definitely get nowhere. Anyway, you can't get to South America in time to do anything.

Vicki stared at me anxiously, "What are you going to do?"

I looked back and smiled, "Relax, I'm okay now. I'm going to call San Francisco."

The Human Freedom Center in Berkeley, California knew all about Jim Jones. It was made up of Jones's ex-cult members who lived with fear but also a determination to expose the sordid affairs of the People's Temple. During my long, frightening, and lonely investigation of Jones they had provided priceless information. They had also been very frustrating. Some suspected me of being a Jones counter-agent. All of us ex-members carried a little remnant of the paranoia Jones instilled in us. We could not get rid of it. I finished my conversation with Berkeley and then hung up.

"It's true," I told her. "They confirmed it. There are several dead and wounded. Listen, Vicki, you may not believe me but that suicide pact is real. I was a part of that cult. It's real. Whatever he says goes. There are going to be thousands of deaths."

I talked to information and then dialed the White House. "Hello [stay calm, I told myself], there's been a shooting in Guyana."

A young man spoke on the other end of the line, "Yes, so what?"

"Well, this will be very hard to believe," I said, "but there is a cult involved in this and they have a suicide pact. If anything on the outside threatens this cult, they'll all kill themselves. There are going

3

to be hundreds of dead bodies tomorrow morning."

The young man at the White House broke into laughter and then, *click!*

I hung up. Vicki stared at me, "What happened?"

"He laughed and hung up on me."

Vicki looked at my untouched iced tea, then back to me, "Well, it was pretty stupid, phoning the White House."

"Yeah," I said. Then I dialed the White House again. "Wait! Don't hang up! Don't hang up! Listen to me," I pleaded. "I'm the man you just talked to. Listen, I've had correspondence with one of the president's aides on this cult. I've been pleading with him to direct the justice department to investigate them. They are involved interstate and international. It's not out of their field. And one of the presidential aides talked to me personally during a trip out here in Oregon and he promised to show the president the information. Look, I know this sounds stupid, but this is for real. A lot of people will be dead. Hello? Are you there?"

There was a long pause before the voice at the White House spoke. "Look, I've got things to do, all right?" *Click!*

I must have looked pitiful. I could see Vicki's face reflecting my own. I dialed the White House again. "You don't understand. There's a madman over there. I've been investigating him for years. Listen, I'm a businessman in Portland, Oregon. I'm not an idiot. I know you don't just call up the president, but

4

put yourself in my shoes. This is going to be a big incident. There will be many ramifications—even political ramifications. The president's wife called Jones up on the platform and shook his hand at a mass rally in San Francisco. The president should be informed, at least informed."

"Okay," the voice at the White House said. "Call the state department."

"But surely you have an aide at the White House, someone who could take the information and make a decision about its importance. That's why I called. There's not much time. I can't just start with a night watchman at the state department and work my way up. Please!"

"Call the state department."

"What's the number? How do I reach them?"

"I don't know." *Click*!

For the third time the White House had hung up on me. I dialed information and reached a night clerk at state. "This is life and death," I pleaded. "I have inside information that might help."

"There's no one here to talk to you," the man said. "I can't get anyone at this hour. Call the FBI."

I hung up and then took a big drink of the iced tea. For the first time since the news bulletin I let out a big sigh and slumped back in my desk chair. I felt exhausted. Vicki began to rub my shoulders and neck. From the other room came cheers from the TV set. David had just killed Goliath. Vicki began to cry now. "I hate to see you this way," she said.

"Vicki," I said, "my mother and my sister are down there. I know what is going to happen. I have to stop it." I slumped on the desk and began weeping. And then slowly I began to get more strength. I felt anger.

Maybe Guyana is too far away, but someone else's mother and sister are in the People's Temple in San Francisco. God, I'll make a deal. I'll get the police into San Francisco to some of those people if you'll get someone else into Guyana and save my mother and sister. Please God. I'll do anything in my power. An hour later I called the FBI.

"There's a madman down there," I explained. The FBI listened patiently to my story.

"Are you sure there's been a shooting in Guyana?" the voice asked.

"Am I sure?" I shouted back incredulously. "You mean you don't even know that?"

"Let me check," he said.

An Agent Rasher returned to the phone this time.

"And there's going to be a mass suicide," I explained. "It will happen in Guyana and it will happen in San Francisco."

"What do you expect me to do?" Rasher asked.

"Get in there!" I shouted. "Break into the People's Temple in San Francisco. I can get you affidavits for probable cause, I can show the interstate connection. Get the FBI in and secure the place, confiscate weapons and poisons. I know where they stash the stuff."

6

"You know we're in a different time zone," Rasher said.

"Yes! But this is an emergency. You've got to get someone into the temple."

Rasher paused and then gave me a telephone number. "This is Mr. Bushnell, Deputy Assistant Secretary to Latin American Affairs. Give him a call."

I reached Bushnell immediately. "You know about the Jim Jones cult and you know about the shooting?"

"Yes," Bushnell replied. "We've set up a command center for Guyana." There was some noise in the background. "Just a minute Mr. Kerns, stand by." He returned to the phone moments later. "We've just got a confirmation. Leo Ryan is dead."

"Listen," I said. "It's not going to end there. Congressman Ryan and the reporters who are dead are only the beginning. Jones will kill them all. He will convince them to die with him. There's going to be a mass suicide!"

My wife looked at me and cringed. I was not articulating very well. I sounded crazy.

"Well, who is this Jim Jones?" Bushnell asked.

I paused—calm yourself, I thought, easy does it. "Jones is a preacher," I said, "and a Socialist. Only in the last few years he's been more Socialist than preacher. He's done a lot of good with drug addicts, with the poor, with people in prison, but he's a demagogue. He has a messianic complex and he

7

rules his followers like God.

"Listen, Mr. Bushnell, I was in the cult. Jones has gone crazy. They do anything he tells them. In a public meeting he ordered a man to pull his pants down and grab his ankles to show his rear to the whole congregation. Then Jones said, 'I had sex with this man and he gave me a rash.' Mr. Bushnell, I'm sorry this is so crude."

My wife shot me a disapproving glance.

"Once his marriage committee decided to break up a couple in love," I explained. "He ordered the girl to have sex with another man before an audience of a thousand. The man's crazy. I'm sorry to have to be so crude but now I'm sure you can believe me that if he says kill yourself, they will do it!"

"Calm down," Vicki whispered. Once again she began to rub my back and neck. "Calm down." Mr. Bushnell waited silently on the line.

"He had public beatings in the church," I continued. "I was in the cult for years. I began to question things and there were some mysterious deaths. Finally a young man was killed. I know he was murdered. He was a teenager and he was carrying thousands of dollars. They tampered with his medical charts. The mother wanted an investigation but they blocked it."

Mr. Bushnell was silent. I felt sick. I was not convincing. I sounded scatterbrained. I was too excited.

"You've got to believe me. I've been investigating

this guy for years. Jones personally threatened to kill me. I've interviewed hundreds of people. I've walked a thousand miles back and forth across San Francisco." Then I remembered, "There was an article in *Newsweek*. You could have researchers get it for you and newspaper accounts in the *San Francisco Examiner*. He was referred to as a murder suspect, and accused of jury tampering.

"Listen, Mr. Bushnell, these people have practiced mass suicide. They rehearse it like a fire drill over and over. If we act now we can save some lives. Please!"

Mr. Bushnell spoke at last. He spoke very softly, "This is really hard to believe."

I sighed from exhaustion. Laughter came from the Johnny Carson show in the other room. It must be really late in Washington, D.C. "Yes, it's hard to believe." I looked at Vicki. She turned away. "Mr. Bushnell, if I were in your shoes I wouldn't believe me either, but what are you going to do? I can get you evidence. There are people like myself who will sign affidavits. We can get probable cause that a crime will be committed and they can break into People's Temple and save some lives."

Mr. Bushnell replied, "I didn't know about this mass suicide thing. We know very little about this whole affair." Then suddenly he snapped, "I'm sorry, I have an urgent call coming in." He hung up.

I looked at Vicki. She had dozed briefly in the other room. Now she stood propped up against the

9

office doorway with another glass of iced tea for me. "Did they know about the mass suicide?"

"No," I admitted. "But Vicki, it's true, honey."

I called the state department back. Mr. Bushnell came on the line. "I've notified the FBI and I gave them your story."

"Okay," I answered. "Here's what we've got to do. We've got to get a warrant and break into Jones's temple in San Francisco and save those people from their leaders. Contact the California State Justice Department. And we've got to get into Jonestown in Guyana."

Bushnell sounded only casually curious, "Why not the San Francisco D.A.?"

"There are Jones people in the D.A.'s office. Jones was under suspicion for tampering with the polls. Look, he's a power broker. He delivered twenty thousand votes to Mayor Moscone and got appointed head of the San Francisco Housing Authority in return. He's got people."

I began to break down. Hold on, don't break, I coached myself. "When I was in San Francisco trying to find my mother, I lived alone, hidden. I went to the D.A.'s office with a big file of tapes and correspondence and gave only them my telephone number. When I got back Jones's people were calling, threatening me and warning that my mother would be chopped to pieces. They had to have gotten my number from the D.A.'s office." That was stupid I thought, I am sounding incoherent again.

10

"Believe me. Call California State Justice. The people at the Human Freedom Center in Berkeley can tell you about the D.A.'s office."

"Okay," Bushnell said. "We'll contact California State Justice."

I hung up, gulped down my iced tea and called the California State Justice. There was no answer. Is my mother dead? There had been no news bulletins. No news is good news. I can't get into Guyana, God. Please take care of my mother and sister. I will get help into San Francisco. I dialed the San Francisco police department. Officer Fourntey answered.

"Did you get a message from the state department?"

"Yes, we did."

"And what did you do with it?"

There was a pause. The officer may have been put off by my directness. "We've given a copy to the D.A. investigation office."

I telephoned the D.A. investigation office. "Did you get the message from Washington, D.C.?" I asked.

"Yes."

"Can you get it to the D.A.?"

"I'm sorry. He's at a birthday party."

"Can't you get his signature? That's all we need. We have probable cause."

"No."

"Do you know what you're doing?" I pleaded. "There is going to be a mass suicide. Don't you

11

believe all this?"

"I'm sorry," he answered.

"Please, we've got to get into People's Temple," I said. There was no response. "All right, all right," I said. "You've been told. If there are dead bodies on the ground your head's gonna roll."

I dialed the state department. "Where's Mr. Bushnell? I've got to talk to him."

"My name's Griffith," a voice said. "Mr. Bushnell is very busy."

"Did he tell you about the suicide pact?"

"Yes, he did," Griffith answered.

"Well, what are you doing?" I asked.

"We're trying to get the pilot and members of Mr. Ryan's team back," Griffith said. "We're going in to find the survivors of the shooting."

"Tell Mr. Bushnell he did not get ahold of the California State Justice like I told him," I shouted hoarsely. "Of all things he went to the San Francisco D.A. I warned him about that. Jones has friends there. It just slows it down. We're running out of time! Please help!"

"I'm sorry," Griffith said. "We are very busy. Hang up and we'll call you back."

I dialed the Human Freedom Center. "What's going on? I'm trying to help. I've been in touch with the state department."

Jeannie answered the phone, "Phil, I don't want you to get involved. Stay out. You're in the way. Stay in Oregon where you belong."

12

"Jeannie, are there any news people involved?" I asked.

"Channel 7," she said.

I dialed Channel 7 in San Francisco. They turned me over to a Steve Davis. "Where's the district attorney?" I asked. "We've got to get the district attorney to sign a document. We can get affidavits to show probable cause that a crime will be committed. We've got to break into the People's Temple. There are going to be some suicides and probably murder. Where's the D.A.?"

"He's at a birthday party," Steve Davis said.

I paused, delighted by what I heard. It sounded to me like Davis understood the situation. It was just a hunch I had. There was a little bit of contempt or cynicism toward the slow-moving bureaucracy in the reporter's voice.

"Can't you use some kind of influence to get that man to sign the document?" I asked. "We've got to get into the temple."

"You're talking about the suicide pact of course?" Davis asked.

"Yes!" I shouted almost joyfully to find someone who believed and understood. "Yes, the suicide pact!" I turned to see my wife standing in the doorway. She was staring at me in bewilderment and confusion.

"It's true," she muttered.

"Vicki!" I shouted. "This man is a San Francisco television reporter. He knows all about the suicide

13

pact. You see, it's true. I'm not crazy!"

"Hello? Sir?" Davis called to me over the phone. "Sir, are you all right?"

"I'm all right," I said. "You don't know how all right I am. Listen, we've got to get police protection for the Human Freedom Center."

"Okay," Davis said. "Let's do this. Let's go to the chief of police. Just skip the D.A. We'll get some police in there."

I hung up. "It's true," Vicki muttered again. I smiled at her. My eyes were bloodshot, my face showed my exhaustion.

"I'm not crazy," I said. "They're going to kill themselves."

Vicki grabbed me and broke into sobs. Her tears washed all over my face and hair. I sobbed and embraced her. "You're not crazy," she said, running her fingers through my hair. "I love you. You aren't crazy. Will you forgive me for not believing you?"

My body shook as I wept. I nodded yes with my head. I could hardly believe it myself. How could I blame her for doubting me? A loud, fuzzy noise roared from the TV in the other room, indicating that the station was off the air. It was Sunday morning in Washington, D.C.

I had talked to White House operators, state department officials and local San Francisco policemen. I had probably spent hundreds of dollars on the telephone. I hadn't slept in hours. And what had I achieved? I had convinced my wife I was

14

telling the truth. I clung to her tightly. It was a victory, but small solace in light of the grim probability that thousands might soon die.

One thing was certain—within the next hours I had to do better, much better. I had to be more convincing. I had to reach the right people. At any time a message could come to San Francisco and Los Angeles. Some prearranged signal perhaps, and mothers would begin killing their children. Tough cultist soldiers would slit the throats of those who attempted escape. The strong would voluntarily drink cyanide. Thousands of people could die. "O God," I prayed, "if my mother and sister are still alive out there, somewhere in the jungle, please keep them safe for me. God, keep them safe!"

# two

## "Tell the D.A. the Party's Over!"

It was very early Sunday morning but I had found new strength. I wiped the tears from my eyes and ordered my wife to bed. "I'm going to beat this thing," I said. "Don't worry."

I called the San Francisco FBI. "Are you aware of what is going on in South America? Do you know about the suicide pact and what could happen in San Francisco?"

"Yes," they answered.

"Can you do anything?" I asked. "There are going to be some murders too."

"No," came the answer. "There's nothing we can do. This is out of our jurisdiction. Only local authorities can handle it."

"And they won't!" I said. "We can't get the district

attorney to sign a probable cause document. Can't you fellows use some of your information to convince the D.A.'s office that this is serious?"

"You've been watching too many movies," he answered. "The FBI doesn't pressure local authorities."

I dialed the San Francisco police and found out that Steve Davis of Channel 7 had also called. They rattled off a bunch of things about murders and suicides. "Yes," I said, "I told you that hours ago."

"Nobody told us anything," he said.

"Oh, yes," I answered angrily. "I told you I've been trying to inform people all night long. No one would listen to me. I guess a TV news celebrity has more credibility than an average citizen. Well, what are you doing?"

"Just relax, mister," he spoke condescendingly. "We've got a command post outside the People's Temple. You want us to go in. Then we'll have to have a warrant. We're observing the thing from the outside."

"Outside?" I exclaimed. "Oh, great, that's just terrific. The only problem is they're going to kill themselves inside not outside! Get a warrant! Get in there!" I hung up on him. It was stupid, I guess, but it was a little revenge for all the people who had been hanging up on me the last few hours.

I called the San Francisco D.A.'s office. They got the affidavits from the Human Freedom Center but the district attorney still wouldn't issue probable cause. "What's going on?" I screamed. "Are you just going to let it happen? Can't you at least protect the children or give people the option to leave? Anything to break down the structure, the control."

"What can we do?" an aide asked me. These are his exact words. "Where would we put 'em all?"

I slammed the receiver down. "Damn!"

Maybe the state department can help, I thought. Once more I was on the line to Washington. "Listen," I said. "Can't you do something?"

"We only handle international affairs," they explained.

"Yes," I countered, "but you have information that could prevent crimes in San Francisco. Couldn't you just share the information with the people out here? You could let them know the seriousness of the situation. You could exert some influence. I mean, if they get a call from the state department they're going to be impressed."

"Just a minute," I was told and then I was given an emergency number to call.

It was the White House again. I started to explain and this time I was transferred to the state security office. "Hold on," I was ordered. Then I was transferred to a secret service agent in the White House. I sensed I was getting close.

"We must get an executive order from the president," I said. "Please wake him up. This is a life and death matter."

"Who gave you this number?" he asked angrily.

"Who is this?"

"Just tell him Phil Kerns, Portland, Oregon!" I shouted back with equal indignation.

"Who?"

"Phil Kerns! Phil Kerns!" I shouted. "Look, can't you wake the president?"

"Yes, I can," he said. "But I won't. I'm a secret service agent. I can't make that decision."

"Okay," I calmed down. "Look, this is a real crisis. It is serious. Who can I talk to?"

"The state department," he answered. "The justice department, the FBI."

I hung up and called back the state department. "This is Miss Cella," a voice said. "I'm in charge here, Mr. Kerns. You don't run the state department. Now, I'm busy and I don't have much time to talk."

"Just a minute lady, please!" I was angry too. What did I have to gain? This was no ego trip. All I wanted to do was save some lives. "Can you or Mr. Bushnell get ahold of the president and tell him he should consider using an executive order. Some law enforcement agency needs to secure the People's Temple in San Francisco. There may be murder and suicide on a mass scale."

Miss Cella was firm. There was no sympathy in her voice. "No!"

"There's no way to direct or encourage or plead with the authorities in San Francisco to do anything?" I asked.

"That's a local matter," she replied.

"But it relates, it relates to international affairs," I insisted. "Guyana is involved, it is interstate, international. The executive branch has reason to become involved. Don't you see, the San Francisco police can't get inside the People's Temple? They are only outside. That means nothing." I felt a new wave of exhaustion hit me. I was afraid I'd faint. I slumped on the desk holding the phone awkwardly. "You're sure?" I asked Miss Cella. "There's no way to get the president?"

"No," she answered sternly. "It can't be done!"

I hung up and for a few minutes I was asleep at my desk. I awakened with a start. Staring me in the face was the special secret service number the state department had given me. I dialed the White House again. I argued. I pleaded, and I soon found myself talking to the same voice I had reached before.

"Please, sir," I said. "I know you are not supposed to wake the president. I know you have rules. I know it is very important to keep schedules and procedures. But, sir, this is not Nazi Germany. This is America where we are free individuals who think and act intelligently. Sometimes we act on our own initiative. Not always, just sometimes and that's our genius as a people.

"Don't hang up! Listen to me." I explained the situation in Guyana and the danger in San Francisco. "Now, you're never going to forget this call. You have a choice. You may lose your job by getting the president of the United States to this telephone to make his decision or you may keep your job and tomorrow morning there will be thousands of murdered children and suicide victims you could have saved!"

There was silence. "Please, sir." I sensed I was getting to him. "You can't hide behind a rule, now. You are not just a part of a machine. You are an individual and you will have to answer for your decision for the rest of your life." Silence. "Sir? Sir? Do you have children of your own? Do you have a sister?"

There was silence. I had been effective. I knew it. It was not what I said as much as the balance between authority and sincerity my voice had struck. This, perhaps the most important phone call I could make, and perhaps the most difficult of all to convince, had been my best performance.

"Sir?" the secret service agent's voice was uncertain. "I want to help. I really, really want to help." He hesitated. "But I can't just break the rules like that."

So close, I thought, so close. Why couldn't I be that convincing with the San Francisco police or the district attorney? Someone who can act immediately. Why should I be so effective when I am pursuing such a long shot. One cannot just telephone the president!

"Boy, I feel sorry for you!" I said. "For once in your life you have an excuse to forget some of that crap and save some people's lives."

"Sir, I'm sorry," his voice was kind, but hardening. "I want to help but this will get me into a lot of trouble. You just don't understand, sir."

I put the receiver down. So close—and yet so far. I began to weep. Vicki was awake again. She came into the office and sat down. "I almost did it," I said with tears rolling down my cheeks. "I was good. I almost got through. I'm on a hot streak. I'm going to the San Francisco police again. I think I can convince them. Pray for me, Vicki!"

The policeman from San Francisco tried to be reassuring. "We are doing everything within our power."

"I want to tell you something," I said. "You tell the D.A.'s office that people are calling up and complaining. If there are dead bodies in there tomorrow there will be some investigations. I'll organize petitions to every agency and newspaper in this country. If you guys blow this, you'll never live it down!"

"Who are you?" he shouted back angrily.

"My name is Phil Kerns."

"Oh, you're just a citizen, huh?"

"I'm just a citizen?" I said. "We citizens are your employers!"

"Well, let me tell you something, Kerns," he said. "If instead of throwing around threats you people would cooperate and assist us we could accomplish twice as much!"

I laughed for sixty seconds. "Sir, I have been trying all night to get someone into the People's Temple to save those people, whether they want to be saved or not. I've been calling your office all night."

"Well, you never talked to me," he said.

"Listen," I said. "If you can get inside it's all over. I've been in this cult. They can't operate with outsiders around. Their little dream would break down. Just get a person in there and everything will be all right."

"We can't get a warrant," he said.

"And where is the district attorney?" I asked.

"I don't know," he answered. "There's something about a birthday party."

"Birthday party," I shouted. "Its six A.M. The party's over! For God's sake, the party's over!" I began to sweat now. I wiped my forehead. "Officer, I've got an idea. You said you want citizens who cooperate. All right, let me tell you a very good way to get in. Have someone contact Archie Ijames. He's the leader while Jones is gone. He's kind of a nice personality. Just talk calmly with him and tell him some crazy people are on your back and that if he wants you to you'll have a few officers walk through the compound so we can tell these people we checked it out. If he invites you in you won't need a warrant!"

"Just a minute," the officer said. There were some clicks on the telephone line. "All right. Give me this guy's name. Spell it very slowly and repeat what you just said."

I finished the conversation and hung up. It was perplexing. Why did he have me repeat everything? Were they beginning to take me seriously?

There were some more phone calls for me to make. The Human Freedom Center had no news. Steve Davis of Channel 7 news was busy. Once more I got the San Francisco police.

"We got in!" he said. He was excited now. "The chief of police went to a Mr. Archie Ijames and a couple of other leaders. Ijames said, 'Come on in. We have nothing to hide.' They went in with reporters and photographers. They were on alert for poisons and weapons. Everything is okay. Kerns? Thanks!"

"Thank you!" I fairly shouted it. "Thank you! Thank God!"

"Just relax," he said. "The place has been secured."

"They got in?" Vicki asked.

I hung up. "They got in!" I said, smiling.

"Oh," Vicki started to cry and then laugh at the same time. "I'm so proud of you," she said.

I jumped up. "They got in!" I shouted. "They got in!" I hugged Vicki and did a little dance around the office. She and I were both laughing and crying and dancing.

"We're going to have a party," she said.

I looked at the clock. "I'll have eggs and toast," I

ordered.

"Yes, sir," she smiled. "I may just fry every egg in the refrigerator!"

I grabbed her and gave her a big kiss. "I love you!"

"And I love you," she said, staring at me with obvious pride.

Vicki returned within minutes. I sat down at my desk and began to feast on breakfast. In between bites I reached a Ms. Betty Kirincch who is counselor of affairs at the state department.

"Bushnell can't talk," she said. "They're in a meeting and they're really going at it. It will be quite awhile."

"Well, please relate to Mr. Bushnell that the San Francisco situation is better. Tell him I am very relieved."

Next, I reached Agent Rasher at the FBI. "Mr. Rasher, San Francisco looks good. The police are in. I know the psychology of these Jones people. San Francisco will be okay. Can you tell me about Guyana? There are going to be some deaths in Guyana."

"Things are pretty heavy now," Rasher said. "We are doing everything we can. Guyanese soldiers are going in. We have some United States agents going in."

"You don't need an army," I said. "Just a few can secure the place. Has anybody actually gotten into Jonestown?"

"I can't disclose that. Listen, Kerns, we

appreciate your calls and your information. You've helped us." He hung up.

"Honey," Vicki called. "Go to bed. You've been up all night."

"One more call," I answered back. I reached Steve Davis of Channel 7.

"We have a reported suicide," he explained. "One woman and three children are confirmed dead. They were members of the cult working in Georgetown. The woman slashed her children's throats and then her own."

"Dear Lord Jesus," I cried. "I know there are more."

Vicki heard me and rushed to turn on the television. I turned on a radio nearby. One hour later a newsbreak came on. An unconfirmed report stated that the Guyanese Army had swept into the remote Jonestown jungle outpost. Hundreds of dead bodies had been found.

There was a horrible knot in my stomach. I felt like I had been stabbed. "O God, have mercy," I prayed. "Please, God."

I reached Mr. Bushnell at the state department. "It's true, isn't it? The news wouldn't confirm it but it's true."

"No," Bushnell said. "It is not true, Mr. Kerns."

"Look," I said angrily. "It's my mother and sister. I have a right to know. Don't lie to me."

"We do know the Guyanese Army has gone in," he said. "But we have no details. Now, we're very busy here." He again hung up.

Two hours later it was confirmed. Somewhere between three and four hundred men, women, and children had lined up for a cup of poison. An eyewitness said parents had squirted it into the mouths of their children and then drank it themselves. There had been some gun play too. Some had been shot. I reached the state department. Mr. Griffith answered.

"We are very, very sorry this happened," he said. "We are very grateful for your calls. Mr. Bushnell is very grateful."

"You know," I paused. "You've been very slow."

"Mr. Kerns," he said. "This place has been a mass of confusion. We've been flooded with calls. Unfortunately, we have a lot of procedural rules."

News items continued to pour in from Guyana. The death toll was now over four hundred. Another three hundred were believed to have escaped into the jungles. Their survival was in doubt. It was a very wild and remote jungle location. I reached my father in Key West, Florida. He was grief-stricken. We had no choice, we concluded. We had to get to Guyana as quickly as possible. They might still be alive.

Once more I got the state department. "My father and I have discussed it. We are going over. There are snakes and piranhas in that jungle. The escaped cult members might be frightened. We might be able to get them out."

Miss Cella came on the line. She was understandably angry. I was a pest, but then if I could save my mother or sister I didn't mind coming off a little obnoxiously to complete strangers in the state department. "Mr. Bushnell is busy and you've interrupted our work!"

Bushnell came on the line, "It won't be possible for you to go to Guyana."

"I can't sit here," I said. "My mother and sister are down there. They are alive!!"

"We have no names of the dead," Bushnell said. "Stand by."

They connected me to a Commander Santa Maria. Was it a code name? A Guyanese official perhaps? I never knew.

"I'm in charge of military transport," he said.

"Well, I want a military hop over," I told him.

"Can't do it," the commander explained. "We are only using experienced people on this."

"Hey, look," I said. "I have my DD214. I am highly trained. I will drag the rivers—anything, anything. I will submit to authority. I can help."

"I don't think it's possible," he answered.

"Please! Please!" I urged.

The commander paused, "I'll check the Puerto Rican shuttle." He was back within seconds. "The next plane leaves in one hour. You can't get in here in time."

Bushnell took over. "Okay, Mr. Kerns. There's a plane full of reporters going over. You can probably make that flight. You can go if you want."

I thanked him, hung up and called Steve Davis, Channel 7. "I'm going over to Guyana. Is there anything I should know? Anything new?"

"Georgetown is cordoned off," he said. "The reporters are being confined to their hotels. Listen, it looks bad. There may be more dead. You'll find out more on your telephone than in a hotel room in Georgetown."

It was Sunday evening. Vicki fed me supper. "I'm not going," I announced. She hugged me.

"Please, get some rest," she said.

"One more phone call," I promised. Once more I reached the state department's command center. "Have they identified any bodies in Guyana?" I asked. "Do you have any names yet?"

"Yes, I do." It was Miss Cella, the tough one.

"Can you confirm the deaths of my mother and sister?" I asked.

"Yes, I do have a confirmation on them," Miss Cella said. "Your mother's name is Penney duPont; your sister Karen has been identified too."

My heart began to beat like a bass drum. I glanced to the wall of my office where a family picture hung. It was mysteriously gone. "How do you know this?" I asked.

"Survivors from the aftermath pointed out bodies," Miss Cella answered. "There was a locked box with passports. We matched the pictures with the bodies."

"My sister's name is Carol." I groped for a shred of hope.

"She was using the name Karen," Miss Cella said. Then she read a description of the body.

"Yes," I muttered softly. "It's her."

"I'm very sorry to report this," Miss Cella said. "I'm sorry I've been so difficult and hard. I don't expect you to understand."

"Miss Cella," I said, "my country was very slow to respond. You'll end up spending millions of dollars to clean this mess up and a few thousand dollars with some immediate action could have prevented it. But you're wrong. I understand. I do understand. What could I expect from you all? It is a pretty far-fetched story. This is something you can't believe until it happens. I just had to try. I had to make the effort."

I hung up, walked into the living room and laid down on the couch. Vicki had been listening from the other room. She came in, sat down next to me and grabbed my hand. We wept together.

The evening news came on. Larry Leyton's face appeared on the screen. I jumped from the couch. "It's Larry! Vicki, remember him? Listen. They're holding him for the murder of Congressman Ryan."

I sat back down, exhausted, angry, and grief-stricken. "You've done all you can do," Vicki said. "It's over. It's all over. Leave it."

"That could be me," I said watching the news story on Leyton. I knew what I had to do. I had spent years investigating Jones. The threat of terror and

31

reprisal had seemed far-fetched to Vicki. She had been more concerned about me, about it becoming an obsession, about me becoming bitter. Now the physical danger loomed before her. What she had thought was my paranoia seemed very real to her.

"Honey, I'm going to have to tell my story. I will not live in fear any longer. You're right. It's over and the story must be told."

"They have millions stashed away," she said. "You've told me about it and now I believe you. Even now they have hired killers to 'get' anyone who talks." She looked at me pleadingly.

"You know what Vicki?" I sat up. "If I had written that book a long time ago this may not have happened. Well, I'm not going to miss this time."

# three

## *"Father Jim Loves You"*

I first began to hear about the People's Temple in 1967 when I was fifteen. My mother had written me some pretty curious letters. It all sounded crazy. If I moved back to her and California she would probably drag me off to her church. Still, I was lonely for her. Growing up with divorcees isn't easy. I had found myself shuttled back and forth between two sets of parents.

The very first night I arrived my mother started in. "Phil, I just want you to meet this man. He's so beautiful. He loves little children. He doesn't care if they're black or white or brown." She laughed, "He even loves the animals."

This is positively weird, I thought.

"He even loves you!" she said. "He's so kind. I've

told him all about you."

For a boy my age, this was pretty corny. I was obviously uncomfortable. Even so, I was prepared. From the letters, I had gotten the impression that something like this would happen. I could handle it. It was still good to be home.

"I told everybody I was bringing my son to church this afternoon," she said. She stood above me, hands on hips, and a beaming smile.

"Church on Saturday afternoon?" I asked. She nodded.

"Mom," I shook my head. "I'm so tired. I just got in." I gave a little laugh, "Anyway, I'm just not the church-going type. You know that?"

"Just come see for yourself," she insisted.

My sister Carol was sitting next to me on the couch. "Phil, she's telling you the truth. Jim Jones is so beautiful. We've never met a man like him before."

I smiled. Carol was so cute. She was a little ten-year-old girl who sounded like an adult. She was probably just parroting something she had heard my mother say. It struck me funny—my mother standing over me, little Carol pleading with me.

"Okay, okay," I threw up my hands in surrender. They cheered.

We drove to the People's Temple in Redwood Valley. The car pulled into a graveled driveway. It looked like any other church except there was no steeple.

The church grounds were filled with people. I was immediately struck by the fact that this congregation was multiracial. Blacks, whites, and Chicanos mixed freely, and everyone was talking.

"Come on, Phil," Carol jumped from the car. "I have so many friends I want you to meet."

It was an unnerving experience, certainly different from the Catholic Mass I was used to.

Carol beamed proudly. Her older brother was finally there. She was rushing around, dragging me from one person to the next. I searched the faces, everybody seemed so happy.

"And inside we have a swimming pool!" she said.

"A swimming pool?"

"Yes! Yes!" She ran on ahead. She's a doll, I thought. Beautiful blonde hair, blue eyes, slender little ten-year-old frame. She was so happy.

There was a swimming pool all right. Children splashed and played. Older women supervised and comforted the kids. There seemed to be much love and concern for each other. It was impossible to separate one family from another. Nearby a band was practicing to a large audience of empty chairs. "Let's take it from the top," the director shouted and off they went again.

Is this the church? I wondered. There was no separation or divider between the auditorium and the swimming pool. In one other room was a long table full of refreshments. Neat little cups of Kool-Aid were lined up. An enormous black woman had taken charge. She was so big that the sight stunned me for a moment and I just watched as her enormous frame floated around. Then suddenly behind her I saw a familiar face.

Ruth was another of my little sisters. She had become a teenager only months before, but she looked like an eighteen-year-old girl. She ran to me and embraced me. "Phil, they brought you! They brought you!" she shouted.

I hadn't seen her in a long time. I remembered her as a little girl and the shock of seeing her as a young woman left me rattled. Carol grabbed one of my hands and Ruth the other. We walked around the church grounds talking constantly.

"That's father!" Carol shouted.

These words startled me since I had just left my father in Key West, Florida. I looked across the compound and saw a large pen with a zoo of barnyard animals. Everything from a horse to chickens wandered around the cage.

"See the man with the black hair?" Carol shouted. "That's father."

I looked back at the man wandering among the animals in the pen. "And why do you call him that?"

"Oh, he loves us, Phil," Ruth said. "He loves us more than our own father."

"Come on!" I was a little angry. "Your father loves you two very much."

Ruth laughed at my anger. "You don't understand, Phil."

36

"Who is he?" I asked.

"Jim Jones," she said. "He's our pastor."

We walked over to the cage. Jones looked up and smiled. He had jet-black hair, the blackest I had ever seen. His face had an olive complexion, with deep dark eyes. It was one of the most handsome faces I had ever seen.

Jones gently stroked the back of the horse and then hugged the animal's neck. He walked over to the chickens and reached out and touched them. They stood quietly, not even moving as he approached. I said nothing, but it was clear that the animals were very much relaxed around him—even attracted by him. It was magical and strange.

He opened the gate and the animals followed him out. People crowded around, especially the children. They touched him or stumbled along pulling at his arms. He walked easily and smoothly through this crowd.

"Where's he going?" I asked.

"That's where he lives," Carol said, pointing to a two-story house behind the church.

The horse and chickens plodded along with the people, following the man with the jet-black hair. It looked stupid and yet it was so remarkable, so uncanny, something that only happened on Saturday morning cartoons. "See," Carol said, "even the animals love him."

"Carol," I said, "I just don't understand."

"Oh, you will," Ruth promised. We picked up our

37

little cups of Kool-Aid and sat down outside. We talked for another fifteen minutes.

"Okay!" a man suddenly shouted. "Let's go inside. Come on everybody!"

People were still laughing, shouting and talking. When we got inside everyone headed for the rows of chairs, but children were still in the swimming pool. I laughed to myself and shook my head. It was strange, very strange.

"I've got to get out of here!" I said.

"No, Phil, please," Carol said, grabbing me.

"I'm just going to the men's room," I lied. "I'll be back. I'll be back."

She hesitated, then decided it would be better psychology just to trust me. "Okay," she smiled.

A tall black man stood with folded arms blocking the exit. I angrily brushed past him. There was a vineyard nearby and a farmhouse across the street. I walked and walked, circling back into the parking lot. I took one look at the old, old automobiles and gave a laugh. They were junkers, falling apart.

Five people stared at me from the church building. I stared back a little indignant at the suspicion in their eyes. One of my mother's friends, a black woman, approached. "Aren't you coming in?" she asked sweetly. "Don't you want to hear Pastor Jim?"

"You mean father?" I asked with a small trace of sarcasm.

"Oh, Phil," she said catching my tone of voice.

38

"You'll understand. Once you get to know him like we do, you'll understand." She led me back into the auditorium. It was crowded now. Carol and Ruth moved down a seat and I sat next to my mother.

There was a roar of conversation. After five or six minutes the back doors opened. A frail, white young man stepped in and stood by the doors. He had a strange look on his face. I would get to know him better in the months to come. He was Larry Leyton. Eleven years later, allegedly at Jones's command, he would assassinate Congressman Leo Ryan.

Jim Jones appeared at the door. He was wearing dark sunglasses. The band struck up. He swept in wearing a long, black robe with a red shirt beneath it. People stood to their feet. The audience broke into singing, "We shall overcome, we shall overcome, we shall overcome someday."

Every eye followed Jones to the stage. There was an electricity, a magnetism. I remembered Jones with the animals. It was all alarming, frightening and yet wonderful!

The band broke into another number. It was triumphant. Jones stood, the audience cheered and applauded. Chills went down my spine. The music stopped and we sat down. I wondered what I was seeing. I've never been with people so excited. I knew they were present for a purpose.

Jim Jones grabbed the microphone. His voice was deep and moving, "Isn't this just wonderful?" he said. "Just think, nowhere else in the world are there people like us. Here we are unashamed. Just as Martin Luther King dreamed. It's come true. Black, white, yellow—unashamed!"

He had power, there was no doubt about it. With the first few words I already knew why these people were here. I wanted more. My attention was fixed. I couldn't even take my eyes off of him.

"Bring the children!" he suddenly shouted. I turned around nervous and confused. "Right now!" he demanded urgently. "I want the children. They need me," he said. "They need my love. 'Suffer the little children to come unto me.' Right now! I need their love."

A tall, black man stepped to the microphone, Archie Ijames, the assistant pastor. "Mothers," he directed, "bring your children. Please bring them right to the front."

Mothers began to pull their children out of the nearby swimming pool. They toweled them down and then sent them scampering off to the front. We had been at the church all afternoon. Some children were sleeping. Mothers carried them to the front in their arms.

Jim Jones held them. The children kissed him and cuddled as near to him as they could. "This is why we're here," he shouted. "It's for these children. It's all for them. We have to work, and work, and work, and we have to stay together for these babies! So they can have a world full of love. A world where there is no hate! A world where there is social equality! A world with racial equality! A world with economic equality!"

The audience cheered, "Yes, father! Yes, father!"

A three-year-old black girl raced across the stage and jumped into his arms. Jones smiled. "Little Tina's been trying so hard to learn this song. She's only three," Jones said. "Only three."

He held the microphone to her. I didn't expect much but it was beautiful. She could not have been better if she had rehearsed for weeks and now, looking back on it, I realize that she probably had. There at the time it seemed so spontaneous and beautiful. A three-year-old girl singing, "We shall overcome." And Jim Jones shouting with kind emotion, "Our dream! Our dream! Our dream!"

It moved me. Something's happening here, I thought. I looked around, trying to isolate a common denominator. But there were children, there were teenagers, middle-aged adults and people so old I thought they would die on the spot. Something's happening all right.

"I give you all the children," Jim Jones said magnificently, as if he had created them or something. "Here they are. The children!" He organized them into a group then put his arms around them. "These are the social egalitarians of tomorrow!"

"Egalitarians." It was a word I didn't understand, but a word I would hear many times thereafter.

I have tried often to remember the sermon, or

speech, or message, or whatever you would call it, that Jones delivered that night. He spoke of the American president and world affairs. Being fifteen years old and naive about politics I did not keep up with his talk, but I do remember the clichés. I would hear them repeated a hundred, a thousand times over.

He spoke about race and economics and nuclear war. "The world will destroy itself. It will happen," he warned. "Greed!" he shouted. And he began to repeat the word until I thought he would never stop. "Greed! Greed! Greed! Greed! Greed!" It sounded ugly and terrible. I felt ashamed. "This imperialist hunger for success is destroying us!" he preached.

"It's a terrible thing," Jones said, "when a black man walks down a street with all those white eyes staring him down. It's an unjust world! It's an unmerciful world!"

"Yes! Yes!" people would shout back. "Yes, father!"

"I tell you there is mercy here in this room!" Jones shouted joyously and with power. "There is justice here in this room! There is love here in this room!" And I knew he was telling the truth. I could just feel the sincerity. There was love here.

"We will fight to the finish," he promised. "Now, we have a letter-writing campaign. This is the month. This is the month. What's the matter with some of you? Your flesh is weak. Our efforts can't die. Turn off those car radios, turn off those television sets. Get these letters to those congressmen.

"Aren't you tired of the pain? Aren't you tired of being stepped on? Then get off your ass. Then turn off that television and do something!"

When Jones used slang or even profanity my mother turned to see how I would react. Once she smiled as if to say, "See, you thought I was dragging you off to some fuddy-duddy old-fashioned thing. Jim Jones is relevant. He's not phony."

Jones looked to the left. The band broke into music. Once more, "We shall overcome." This time Jones held the microphone and sang it loudly. They repeated it over and over. People stood up. The lady in front of me started to cry. She was a big black woman. "Oh, Father Jim," she cried. "Father Jim. How we love you, Father Jim."

The crowd was in a joyous frenzy now. Some were clapping, some were jumping, some were dancing. My sisters and my mother mixed right in. I was ashamed of them all and quite turned off.

Jones himself was happy, jumping, and dancing. I couldn't believe it. That man is excited. Eventually the band stopped. A bit breathless, everyone began to wind down.

"What a glorious day here in the Redwood Valley," Jones said. "You people don't know what a future you have in store for you. This is the cornerstone," he shouted. "This is the cornerstone! You and I here tonight. They'll speak about us for years to come. These are historic days. This is the beginning of real socialism, real equality! Aren't you glad? Isn't it exciting to be a part of this?"

There were peaks and valleys throughout a Jim Jones performance. The crowd would be worked into a frenzy and then slowly relax only to be brought to their feet again with thundering applause and shouts. It left one exhausted.

"We have some new guests," Jones announced. He sat down in a chair and received a glass of water from one of the workers. Archie Ijames took over.

"Betty is here," Ijames announced in a calm, broken English. "This woman was a drug addict. Father Jim just touched her. Just one touch. She had no withdrawal. Here she is today, never again needing heroin. Never again needing the lie of the needle."

The woman wailed, "Oh, oh. He came to me. He touched me. Oh, I can't believe it. Oh, thank you, Father Jim! Thank you, Jim." Betty was crying. In my youthful, fifteen-year-old mind it looked real. She had no reason to put us on. Betty told her whole story, how she was taken to the drug rehabilitation center, how Jones appeared.

I was stunned. This is a miracle! He just touched her. No withdrawal.

Archie encouraged her, "Wonderful, wonderful." There were cheers, applause and shouts.

The band started playing again. "We shall overcome." That in itself was so corny, so obviously an attempt to work on our emotions that I felt insulted but at the same time a tear was rolling down my cheek. It was pretty hard not to believe Betty. She believed it herself. She was so happy; the fear and the shame was behind her. People jumped up and embraced her, others reached out to touch.

Jim Jones sat in his chair smiling out to us. He looked radiant. He reached his hand out toward Betty.

Archie restored order. "Now, we have another guest here," he said in broken English. I had to strain to understand him. "We want you to meet Penney duPont's son, Philip Kerns. Philip has been through a lot of pain. He needs us. I give you Philip Kerns."

Mother started to the front. "Come on," she said.

"No," I protested. "No, mother. I don't have anything to say."

"I just want them to see you," she urged.

Now there was applause in rhythm demanding my appearance. Deciding it would be less embarrassing to respond than rebel, I followed my mother to the front.

"Oh, I'm so happy!" she grabbed the microphone. "I'm so happy. I have my son. He's so talented." She smiled proudly. "He plays the guitar." I could have crawled under the stage but Jim Jones picked right up on it.

"Give him a guitar," he ordered. "Play us a song, Phil."

They applauded. "Yes, yes, play something."

I thought I was in the twilight zone. "I really don't have anything appropriate to play," I mumbled.

"Just play anything, Phil," Jim Jones spoke so kindly. "Play us something you like."

It's a strange thing. I had always wanted to entertain with the guitar. For a fifteen-year-old kid, I was pretty good, but there were never any opportunities. I had only met these people that day and there I was.

I played and they applauded. From my seat I had been looking at the back of their heads, now from the front I saw their faces. They were all smiling the same strange eerie smile.

Jim Jones stood, and laughed, and nodded. On the way back to my seat an old man grabbed my hand and squeezed it. He had sensed my fear, my uncertainty.

Jones stood at the podium. The mood of the audience suddenly shifted. Perhaps they had taken their cue from Jones, some facial expression or movement that I had missed while walking back to my seat. He removed his sunglasses, laid them on the podium, and dug his fingers into his eyes. There was silence, absolute silence.

"Yes, yes," Jones started to repeat. It was as if he were in a trance. "I see something. Yes, yes, there it is. It's becoming more clear now. I see a picture on a wall. It's a painting. There is a bowl with fruit in it. There is a crucifix on the other wall."

The whole thing sent chills down my spine.

Moments later he began naming names. Of course, I can't remember the exact names but it would go something like this.

"There's a black woman crying," Jones would say. His face became contorted as if he were in pain too. "She is hurting inside. I see an old toaster in the kitchen. It is the old-fashioned kind that opens on the sides. The woman is crying. There is a telegram. It says, it says Alice Johnson has died! Is there anyone here who knows Alice Johnson?"

A black woman from the audience screamed out, "Oh! Oh, God!"

"Oh, I'm sorry," Jim says gently. "Apparently Alice is going to depart from us." Jones jumped off the platform and raced to the black woman. People gathered around her.

"Yes, Alice is going to depart from us," he said. "She was a good woman. A kind woman." The old black woman just sat there nodding her head at everything Jones said. Tears were streaming down her face.

"All right everybody. Let's gather around," Jones ordered. "Let's cry out to this woman, let's reach out to her." They crowded around her. Some stretched their hands toward her like they do at revival meetings.

Jones silenced the commotion. "I want you to know something," he said. "Everything's going to be all right!" He looked at the black woman. "I want you to know that I love you. I've always loved you."

47

"Yes, Jim," she nodded, still crying.

He returned to his trance. "Buckley, I keep getting the name Buckley. Your name's Buckley?"

"Yes, yes Jim," she was nodding her head violently as Jones narrowed in on the situation.

"And who is Alice?" he asked. "A friend?"

"Yes," she exploded into sobs. She sounded like a little child.

"Did you know that Alice was going to die?" he asks.

"No, Jim. Oh, no, Jim."

"I won't let it happen!" Jones shouted, his voice vibrating in the rafters. Nearby a little child with a blanket awakened and sat up on the floor. "She won't die. I give Alice back her life! I won't let it happen!"

The Buckley woman was hysterical. She began kicking the floor violently and screamed out, "Oh, Jim, Father Jim! Thank you, Father Jim!" The audience shouted. Buckley was on her feet hugging and kissing all over Jim. He stood calmly in the storm of voices and people.

I was scared stiff. I was shocked. My eyes riveted to him. This man could really see things. It was real. Something was happening here. My body broke out in a sweat. I was afraid. I wanted to run, yet I was curious. I wanted to stay.

"Mrs. Buckley, dear," Jones said. "I want you to know, I love you."

"Yes, Jim. Yes, Jim."

"I want you to know that I know about the pain in

your back. I know how hard it has been on you. And Mrs. Buckley, I'm going to heal you now. Right now!"

Buckley screamed and wailed and threw her hands in apparent joy.

"All it takes is faith," Jones coached. He walked backward down the aisle toward the stage. "Come on, just believe," he said.

She followed him down the aisle with a little entourage of her friends in tow. I was in awe, total awe. My mouth was opened. I was staring.

"Just believe!" Jones shouted. The woman was sobbing, walking slowly to him. Suddenly, Jones leaped back to her. His eyes were so sad and tearful. He was moved. He grabbed her hand and pulled her to his bosom. "Don't cry!" he begged. "It's okay. It's okay. Alice has been saved. She will live. You need to be healed, Mrs. Buckley."

"Yes, Jim, yes, Father Jim!" She fell on her knees before him. "O father, O father."

"Stand back up! You don't need to kneel before me!" Jones said humbly. "Now turn around." He poked her up and down her back and then sides. She screamed.

Jones shouted. "Feel that?"

"Yes, Jim!"

"Bend over," Jones commanded. She reached out to touch her toes. Jones moved all around her, his robe flapping like a giant eagle's wings. "This time, no pain," he shouted. "I will touch you. The power of the spirit, the spirit will heal you."

"Yes, Jim! Yes, Jim!" she wailed.

"You have to have faith!"

"Yes, Jim! Yes, Jim!"

"When I touch you no more pain! No more pain!" he screamed. Then he slapped her on the side.

"Thank you! Thank you, Father Jim!" she shouted.

"No pain," Jones said.

"No pain," she responded.

"Bend over," he ordered. "Wave your hands!"

Buckley bent over and stood up and waved her hands and started jumping up and down. Jim joined her. They held hands and jumped. She had tears all over her face. "No pain! No pain! No pain!" she shouted.

The audience went berserk. Everyone started shouting and jumping. Jim moved calmly back to the stage. The crowd moved in to crush him, pawing all over him. The band broke into music. Jones retired to his seat on the stage. A worker slipped him another glass of water. The crowd receded. There was a five-minute pause as we all caught our breath.

A tall, muscular, black man walked center stage. He must have been participating too because he was breathless. "We have so much to be thankful for," he said. "I'm glad we have people like Jim Jones who can speak the truth. I'm so glad we've got a man who is not afraid. A man who can speak to anyone. A man who can make the president listen! A man who can make the kings bow!" There were cheers.

"I'm proud to be here!" he shouted. "I'm glad to be a part of this movement. I'm going to sing a song I've written for you."

It was a song from the heart. I can't remember the lyrics but they expressed the pain of prejudice and injustice and the dream of equality. It was a moving melody. People were crying. I wondered, what would compel this man to write such a beautiful song? This man is sincere, I thought. When he finished, there was a standing ovation. The chairs squeaked on the floor as everyone stood. People were insane with joy. I found myself clapping and shouting. I didn't even understand all of the lyrics, but I felt moved by something deep within me.

The black singer broke into sobs and went over to Jim. They embraced. Jim cried too. It struck me, the black man looked big enough to have broken Jim Jones in two but he seemed like a little boy, like putty in Jones's arms.

Then something happened which in that context seemed absurd. I've often thought of that first meeting. After a thousand hours of Jim Jones the moments melt together and are hard to isolate and identify. But that first meeting has remained clear. While the audience was still choking on their tears from the black man's song, Archie Ijames stepped awkwardly to the microphone. "Jack Beam is going to read the list of those who have had birthdays this month," he said. And with Jim Jones still holding the big black singer, another man grabbed the microphone.

Jack Beam was a portly, slightly bald white man, and one of the most powerful leaders of the People's Temple. "Are you glad to be here?" Beam shouted, like he was leading a pep rally.

"Yes!!" the audience yelled back, some still wiping the tears that came during the song.

"Well, I am too," Beam said. "I want you to know I'm proud. Are you proud to be a part of this great socialist movement?"

"Yes!" they responded, enthusiastically.

"Are we united?"

"Yes!"

"Now, I'm going to read a list of those people who have birthdays this month," Beam said. "Hold your applause until I've read them all. We don't believe in someone off alone celebrating his birthday." Beam read the names, people walked forward, the band played Happy Birthday and I sat back once again trying to figure out what kind of church this was. Meanwhile Archie Ijames returned to the stage.

"Okay, we want you to know we've got a lot of work to do," Ijames said. "We've got these kids in Santa Rosa College. We need doctors and nurses for our medical missionary operation, and we need help in our drug rehabilitation program. We need money for the stamps," he said.

Ah, the offering, I thought.

"We've got a lot of mail," he said. "We're sending

out letters to congressmen. We have friends, we have mayors and legislators out there, but they need our letters. They believe in the socialistic dream. They believe in us. They are on the front lines."

Now the people started cheering Ijames. He had none of the charisma of Jones and none of the macho-enthusiasm of Beam. It seemed as if anybody could have excited the crowd. "We're going to do it!" they shouted back.

Archie Ijames nodded in the direction of Jones. "You don't know our father. You don't know how hard he works. He tries so hard." Ijames choked up tearfully. "He gets three hours of sleep some nights. He's on the phone all the time. He's contacting people in all areas of government. He's trying to help. He's trying to help." Ijames broke down for a few seconds.

"He helps the poor," Ijames said. "He helps the sick. He raises the dead!"

Raises the dead? I thought. Yet, I remembered the old Buckley woman. There seemed to be no doubt, Jones could see through walls.

"You aren't just giving," Archie said. "You are a part of this dynamic movement of truth. As the plates are passed back and forth we will sing that song once more."

It was "We Shall Overcome" and as they sang Jim Jones sat quietly with his head bowed in humility. Now I understood! Now, my mother's letters made sense. Now, I understood my little sisters.

By the time the service ended it was eleven o'clock at night. We had been at the People's Temple all afternoon and evening. We piled into an old, beat-up 1962 Falcon and drove out of the Redwood Valley.

"What do you think, Phil?" mother asked.

"Well, I've never seen anything like it," I admitted.

"Tell me how you feel," she insisted. I just shrugged, keeping all my feelings to myself.

"Honey, we're very busy here," she explained. "We've got another service tomorrow. Jim Jones is going to speak again."

Oh, no, I thought. The service had been six hours! Think of it. Six hours! At the same time I was curious.

We arrived at my mother's little home and she herded all of us into the kitchen. We raided the refrigerator. Mom sat writing her own mother a letter. Suddenly she broke into tears, throwing her letter into the trash.

"What's wrong, mom?" I asked.

"I've been hurt all of my life," she said. "Men have stomped on me and abused me. I've worked so hard just to support you kids." She sobbed, "I feel like I've really let you down, Philip."

My mother was a beautiful woman. Her face was gentle and her personality was vibrant. I pulled her letter out of the trash and though it was written to my grandmother, not me, my mother did not protest as

I read it.

She had written about Jim Jones, pleading for her mother to understand. "He fills an empty spot in my life," she had written. "I really feel like he's going to help my son. Please, mother, try to understand. Jim Jones is such a wonderful man. I'm so thankful my son's here."

I looked up at my mother. "Hey, I understand."

"Oh, you do?" she said and she hugged me tightly. We cried on each other's shoulders. She told me she loved me. I felt so good. I had been away from her too long.

My sisters gathered around to calm her. "Don't cry, mama. It's going to be okay. Jim Jones won't let anything happen to us." We all comforted her.

She stopped her sniffling. "I don't want to feed you all beans," she said. "I just want to take care of you."

I was tired, very tired. Yet, when we finally got to bed I lay restless. I was troubled. Maybe these fears are unrealistic, I finally concluded. Jones was a man who loved people. He was a man who cared about justice. He was a man who talked about faith and hope. It was all exhausting and quite bizarre but a lot of good could come out of it. Certainly there could be no harm.

# four

## *Jim Jones, False "Profit"*

It was decided that I needed a male example, so I was farmed out to the Archie Ijames household. They were a black family who took me in like an adopted son. We went everywhere together. Sometimes it meant hauling lumber, sometimes it was concrete work. Archie seemed to be a sincere and kind man.

I was not especially committed to the Jones family. I thought of it as a temporary affair. It would pass. My mother would get another kind of job and our lives would turn to a different routine. However, events proved otherwise.

Attending the local high school was a traumatic experience. People started to talk about me arriving at the school each morning with Papa Ijames's black daughters. Soon I was being shoved up against my locker with angry shouts of "nigger lover!"

If anything drove me into the Jones family it was that kind of harassment. I found myself defending blacks. I was articulate. Memorized paragraphs from Jones's sermons gushed forth from me, astonishing teachers and confusing my classmate tormentors. "You're ignorant," I would shout back. "You don't even know what you're talking about." In most cases they didn't even know the names of the congressmen, let alone the issues.

One night Archie Ijames stayed up until early morning telling me stories of persecution and prejudice. He was willing to forgive the white man. I went to my bed and cried.

Lil, a young teenage, black girl, became my closest friend. It was puppy love, I suppose, but Mama Ijames, Archie's big, fearsome wife, thought it was cute and she encouraged me.

At church, I found myself clapping and shouting with the others. The miracles began to increase. Instead of two or three a night, there were hours and hours of them. Blind people could suddenly see, cancers were pulled out of people's throats, cripples walked out of their wheelchairs.

Jones's prescient abilities increased. He saw automobile accidents before they happened. Once a home burned to the ground. Jones had prophesied it days before. It was only much later that I realized that all these miracles were not genuine.

"I want you to know you are hearing the truth," Jones would shout. "The whole truth. Nowhere else can you hear the whole truth. No one else will tell you."

I believed it. Others were saying he was God. As early as 1963, Archie Ijames had told Bonnie Thielman, one of the Jones household, "The only god I believe in is Jim Jones."

The transfers of property and the financial exploitation of members had already begun. As a teenager I was not much interested in "power of attorney" or "transfer of title" documents. All I remember was the shifting people.

When old people joined the family several couples would be assigned to live with them and "help take care of the work." The extra homes were evidently sold. We had at least five elderly people living with us in the Archie Ijames household. Did they have homes which the People's Temple took over or were they just abandoned old people?

Even when I began to hear tales of the exploitation of people, I did not become disillusioned. What better cause existed? In the afternoons Jones would telephone Archie Ijames. They often talked about money. When there was excitement or joy, I was pleased too. On one such occasion Ijames hung up, turned around and saw me listening. He gave me a stern look. I was hurt. I was a member of the cause. They could trust me. My mother lived in a shack giving 25 percent of her income. We all believed. They had nothing to fear. Jones was dad; we were just his kids.

If at that time there were no fears within the family, there were certainly fears without. Jones's preoccupation with the nuclear threat became hysterical. We studied maps, locating spots that would be safe when the holocaust came. Jones ranted and raved from the stage but his logic was good. It was not only good; it was convincing.

Then there was our own United States government. Everyone was talking about the courage of Jones. How could he expose such corruption and get away with it? Everyone feared a Jones assassination plot. Rumors circulated that several attempts on his life had been made but that his prescient gift had protected him. He was our superman, our messiah, battling the generals and armies of the whole nation.

Churches in the area were hostile toward us. Jones's reaction was ruthless. Once he marched into the sanctuary of another church. Interrupting the service, Jones pointed to the pastor on the platform. "You molested one of our girls and you claim to be a man of God!" The probably innocent pastor looked stunned and guilty.

My mother was told to witness against a Rev. Ross Case. Case was a Disciples of Christ minister and an old Indianapolis friend of Jones. He had preceded him to California. Mother was supposed to implicate Case in some kind of homosexual affair. It was all false. I didn't hear about it until later but it came as no surprise. The cause was the most important thing. Over and over Jones told us, "The end justifies the means."

Did not Sir Winston Churchill say that in wartime, "Truth is so precious that she should always be attended by a bodyguard of lies"? Well, we were at "war."

I'll never forget one particularly dramatic evening. Jones stopped in the middle of his sermon and fell into a trance. "The FBI is coming," he announced. "I see them coming. They don't believe in us. They will do anything to destroy us." He moaned and acted crazy.

A few of the more skeptical members said Jones was not well rested. The fanatics were not shaken, however. "Jones sees through walls," they said confidently. "If Jones saw something, it has to be real!"

The next night Jones began his moanings again. This time a shotgun exploded outside. "Hit the floor!" a security guard shouted. The big audience was under the chairs immediately. There were moans and cries of anguish.

"Hush!" Jones commented calmly. "Quiet. I can see them outside. Our own security men are chasing them through the parking lot." The audience calmed down, listening to Jones's running commentary. "They're escaping in a car. It looks like a blue Mercury. It's an old car. Everything is okay! Stay calm!"

Moments later, Larry Leyton came running in with a shotgun in his hand. "We ran them off!"

"We don't know who it was," another security man shouted. "They were driving an old, blue Mercury."

There were gasps from the audience.

"Hush!" Jones ordered and we were kept on the floor a short time more.

Was it a plot to assassinate Jim Jones? Most of us felt it was. We reasoned that the U.S. government feared he would become a world leader.

Only days later we were struck again. This time they were closer. Their guns blew out a window of the church!

One night I overheard a Jones telephone call. Archie had a habit of repeating everything Jones said. It was as if he were checking his orders to make sure. It had the effect of allowing an eavesdropper to hear both ends of the conversation.

Jones was talking about the government and how it could freeze bank accounts and about the growing threat from the courts. It was necessary to have money available in cash. Large, large sums of money—international currencies and gold. I crouched near the doorway, listening carefully. They needed some hideouts—several different hideouts. They were to be stockpiled with cash.

Weeks later we began to hear startling news from the pulpit. We were told we had a cave—a refuge for when the nuclear holocaust would come. Our cave was stockpiled with food and money. We planned to inherit this country. The rest of the world would perish. We would be the survivors! "Thank you, Jim. Thank you, Father Jim!" we shouted. I remembered the telephone call and I wondered.

My disillusionment—or awakening—began with the construction of a pulpit. Jim Jones used only a podium. It was decided that he should have a pulpit. Archie Ijames ordered me to work. I was happy, even thrilled at the opportunity. Just imagine—I was going to high school, and volunteering many hours a day for the People's Temple. There was not much time for this project.

"I'm taking wood shop at school," I said. "I can do it!"

Archie bought the finest hardwood and plywood. There was a table saw behind his house. We worked painfully and skillfully.

Jones wanted it in a hurry. It took us only a week.

The last days of our work were frantic. Jones needed the pulpit for a special service in San Francisco.

"Oh?" I asked. "Will this be the San Francisco pulpit?"

"Jim wants this one in Ukiah and San Francisco both," Ijames said.

"But I don't understand," I said. "Why can't he use a different pulpit in each temple?"

"No," Ijames was adamant. "We have to have the

same pulpit both places."

We had finished and it was beautiful. I stood admiring our creation when Archie suddenly returned with a small wooden frame. It was a border which wrapped around the top, approximately five inches high. I had never seen anything like it. It destroyed the looks of the pulpit and was entirely unnecessary.

"Jim isn't going to want that," I said. "It looks awful!"

"Yes, Phil," Ijames replied. "Jim wants it this way."

"But that's so high." I motioned with my hands, "Won't he want it down here? It is so awkward."

"This is the way he wants it! This is the way he wants it! All right?" Ijames seemed a little perturbed at me.

I didn't care. I was so proud of my work. We hauled it into the church and everyone patted us on the back. "Good job! It's about time Jim had a pulpit."

The disillusionment came slowly, like some creeping thought that slipped back even after I had chased it away. Jones was always getting notes, little messages passed to him during the services. There were plausible reasons. Business had to be carried on and when the meetings lasted six hours, business sometimes had to be conducted right on stage. Maybe someone left their automobile lights on? Maybe the PA system was too loud? But did the notes have anything to do with Jones's prescient gift?

Were they slipping him information? Did the five-inch border keep our prying eyes away from his script?

That was a terrifying thought—what if I was wrong? It was a thought that could be dangerous. If Jones could actually read your mind, then he could see your doubts. I had not yet crossed him but I had cringed at the holy wrath he could unload on others. As of yet there were no beatings at the Redwood Valley People's Temple. In San Francisco they were just beginning, but long before the beatings, Jones had possessed an intimidating power that left its victims shaking. We had seen him point his finger at strangers who would promptly fall over, apparently dead.

My doubts caused me great anxiety and guilt. What difference would it make if there was professionalism in Jim Jones's stage personality? What difference would it make if some of his acts were phony? "The end justifies the means." The cause was everything.

To say we all worked hard would be an understatement. When Jones spoke in San Francisco we all rode the buses in from Ukiah. I spent hours walking the streets, passing out flyers. "Go see Jim Jones. He is a wonderful man, a wonderful healer. He doesn't just talk about equality, he is doing something."

The long hours and tight discipline left me exhausted. I was angry too. I suddenly realized I had no friends or contacts outside the family. There was no money, no allowance, no privacy. Such idealism in a teenager was too demanding. I was rebellious and since the family was my authority, that's where I directed my anger.

I often passed through the rooms of the elderly people who lived with us. One day I spotted some money on a dresser and scooped it up. I heard the floor squeak under the weight of big Mama Ijames. I turned in fear but she walked by casually. If she had seen me she would have said something. The old woman sleeping in the bed was senile. She wouldn't even remember her money when she awakened. It was only a few dollars but it promised me some freedom. The next school day I will not return home immediately, I thought. I will pause for a while in some of the Ukiah stores. I will not stay long enough to arouse suspicion—just a few moments.

That Saturday afternoon, we arrived at the temple. I was walking cheerfully across the gravel parking lot when Jim Jones appeared. He startled me. I felt a little guilty because of the money in my pocket, but even beyond that, I was in awe of Jones. I avoided him.

"Phil, there's something I want to tell you." He spoke kindly. "I saw you take that money off the dresser. I saw you. Put it back! I want to forgive you." He walked off.

I couldn't believe it had happened. I broke into tears. Archie Ijames walked up behind me. "He told me, Phil." Archie spoke softly. "It'll be all right. Jim loves you. Just put it back." That night I lay in bed shaking. This had been no note hidden on a pulpit. Jim Jones could see through walls, I thought.

For several days I hid in the big audience, trying to remain as inconspicuous as possible. Even a look from Jones set me on edge. My little sister Ruth noticed my apprehension. One day we had a long conversation. We talked about the Jones family, about the beautiful children.

"He can see through walls," I told her.

"I'm beginning to doubt," Ruth said. She sat up excitedly. I could tell she was giving me information which she had longed to share with someone she could trust. "I saw the nurses with a phony cancer. They were carrying it around before the service."

"What?" I was stunned. "I don't believe it. Ruth, don't be a traitor. He could be listening to us right now."

"Maybe you're right," she said. She looked frightened—not by Jim Jones's supposed omniscience as much as the possibility of me turning her in. She sat nervously wringing her hands. "Maybe I didn't see what I thought I saw." She gave me a worried glance and then added, "One of the girls in the office overheard Mama Ijames talking to Jim on the phone. She told Jim you had taken some money off a dresser." She eyed me hard. She suspected Jim had scared me with the information.

Was Ruth telling the truth? Mama Ijames had been nearby when I stole the money. Coincidental?

Maybe my pulpit theory was right. Maybe they do feed Jim information. Maybe we all had been duped. Maybe we were all the fools of Jim Jones and the ten or twenty in his inner circle. "What's this about the cancer?" I asked.

Ruth shrugged, still a little fearful, wondering if I were only baiting her.

"I've got to know!" I said angrily. "What about these healings? Are they fake?"

"Well," she paused. "I just said I saw a piece of meat wrapped up in a towel. One of the nurses had it, carrying it around before service. She put it in her purse."

"And you think this is all fake?" I asked. "Please, Ruth."

"Yes." She was suddenly fearless. "Yes, they are fake—and the gunshot through the window. It was all set up."

"Don't, don't!" I put my hands to my ears. I wanted to hear what she had to say, but if Jim Jones was watching I didn't want him to think I believed it.

Several days later Jim Jones's wife called. She was coming by to pick me up. Why? I could not imagine. We were in the middle of one of our letter-writing campaigns. Marceline was a quiet, humble woman. She was beautiful, with a charming smile. Ruth and I had often talked about her compassion for the children and her devotion to her husband. Did she really know what was going on?

I ran to the car. "Get in, Phil. Go with me

downtown. We have to go to Tim Stoen's house."

I jumped in the car. "What's going on?"

"It's Jeanette, your sister," Marcie smiled, happy to be able to scoop me on the news." She has come in from Florida." I was anxious to see Jeanette and to tell her all about Jim Jones.

Tim Stoen was the assistant district attorney of Mendocino County. His big, two-story house was now filled with members of the family. Jeanette and I embraced. She looked puzzled. I had indoctrinated her just as my mother had me. "Now we are all together. Mom, Carol, Ruth, you, me and Jim Jones."

Marcie didn't allow us much time. "Let's go. Your sister's tired," she said. "You'll have plenty of time. We need you back at the letter-writing campaign."

Marceline drove us back to the little town of Ukiah, while I pumped her with questions. "What's it like being married to Jim Jones?"

"Oh, Phil," she said. "He's such a kind man, such a loving man."

I just stared at Marcie. She was so devoted to her husband. Rumors of Jones's promiscuity in the family were only beginning at that time. I hoped they weren't true. "And why did you adopt all the children?" I asked.

She looked at me with surprise. "Our children are everything to us. We are giving our whole lives for our children." Her Korean daughter was in the back seat. Marcie looked through her rear-view mirror. "And not just the children we have adopted but all the children in the family."

Marcie was kind. She seemed approachable. The harsh terror tactics of our little society seemed unreal in her presence. "Marcie, are all of these healings real?" I asked.

"Phil!" she was obviously caught off guard. "Yes, of course they are real. Jim has a gift!" She seemed absolutely sincere. Either she believed it, or she had convinced herself, or soft and beautiful as she was, she was just as ruthless in her ambitions as her husband.

"Are you sure, Marcie?" I was surprised at my persistence. All of us loved her. We had heard the stories of their life in Indianapolis. When Marcie had walked down the street with her adopted black child, people had spit on her. The Joneses were light years ahead of their day. But now there was exploitation of people taking place. The cause seemed shaken. How was Marcie involved? Does she understand? Does she approve? We were all confused about her.

She looked hurt and perturbed by my question. "Some people in our community like to smear Jim," she answered. "People will talk to you, Phil; they'll try to shake your loyalty. But if they only knew how hard Jim works. How very hard. There's nothing selfish about Jim Jones."

Marcie looked over at me for a moment. "Phil, you're just a part of us. We're so blessed to have such a large family, with children all over the world. We have such beautiful children. Phil, someday you're going to play a very important role in our family."

Her Korean daughter did not say a word throughout the conversation.

By the end of the week we were back in San Francisco. I spent the afternoon passing out flyers and promoting Jim Jones. The People's Temple services were different now. I found myself analyzing their techniques, imagining how Jones operated. Sometimes it defied any explanation, but then again, he had been doing this for years. I was only now trying to catch on. I looked with contempt at the messengers who slipped little notes on the pulpit I had built.

Still, though, I was out on the street arguing with blacks and whites who were passing by, praising Jim Jones. "Our god you can see and touch."

One weekend after an exhausting night, a friend and I were bedded down with a poor black family that was ruled by a large black woman. The hour was late and we would only have a few hours to sleep but she wanted to keep us up talking about Father Jim. I glanced around her little apartment. Pictures of "our god" were plastered everywhere. One large black-and-white glossy in a cardboard frame served as a shrine. A candle burned in front of it.

I had been in the family only a couple of years but I already had had my fill of Jones. I gratefully grabbed a blanket and curled up on her filthy floor while she and my friend talked on.

She was a weird, crazy woman. She evidently believed everything Father Jim said. For a few terrible moments she brandished a butcher knife in my friend's face, demanding that he admit he was really a traitor. Why I escaped her interrogation I'll never know. Maybe I was too relaxed to be an FBI agent. Maybe she had seen me around before.

I was only seventeen years old. I did not appreciate or understand the word "paranoia." When I discovered it years later I would nod to it politely like an old friend. We were now beginning to live in a world of fear. Not only without but now within. The good old days were gone. We feared Jones. We feared his spies who were all around us. We feared our government. We feared ourselves. I had a wonderful thought that night, as I was curled up in my dirty blanket. I don't have to stay. I can get out of this thing!

# five

## *Escape from People's Temple*

I was suspicious about Maxine Harpe's suicide. She was a kind, nice woman even though she and her lover, Jim Randolph, often fought. Randolph was one of Jones's most trusted henchmen, assisting throughout the services. Once I caught on to the operation, I could spot Randolph as one of the men who helped stage the healings.

The days before her death Maxine looked harassed. Her eyes darted from one person to the next. Once she stopped by during our big mailing campaign. She stared at me like I was the devil. I knew she liked me so I couldn't imagine what I had done.

"What's wrong, Maxine?" I asked.

She broke out of her trance and smiled at me.

There was a look of despair and fear in her eyes. I recognized it because I had the same feeling inside.

Days later, Maxine's body was found. They said she had hung herself right in front of her little children.

"It was murder," my sister Ruth told me.

"Oh, no," I protested. "Listen, Maxine looked troubled and worried all week. I'm not surprised by her suicide."

"She was worried because she knew something," Ruth answered.

"What?" I asked. "What could she have on them?"

"I don't know." Ruth looked away. "I'm getting all this information from my girl friends. I don't know what to believe."

"But why?" I asked. "Why would Jim Jones have anything to hide?"

"Money!" she answered quickly. She was surprised I wouldn't see it so obviously. "There are millions of dollars in this operation. That I know. Can't you see it, Phil? All these people are signing over their homes. They're giving up all their land. He's taking watches and jewelry in the offerings now. This isn't socialism."

"Yes, but they make him sound so humble," I answered. "They say he uses orange crates for a bed stand."

Ruth only shrugged. "I'm not staying around here."

"I'm not either," I admitted. "Eventually I'm

going. But what about mother? What about Carol?"

Ruth didn't answer me. I suspected she had talked to them and been rebuffed. But Ruth had a lot of nerve. If I were going to go I would have to take mother and Carol with me. But to convince them of fraud and exploitation, I would need more than a teenager's rumors. I needed solid evidence.

A high school teacher gave me a good lead. He explained about incorporation and titles to homes and how available the documents were to the public. Unfortunately, I was seen talking to him. Fraternizing with an outsider was no small sin. While at school some contact was necessary, but we spied on each other to "insure our loyalty to the cause."

They came down on me hard. Archie Ijames acted hurt. Why should I have to talk to a teacher about a problem even if it did relate to my studies? Mama Ijames dropped a little bit of fear into me. Jones stared me down that very night in the service. I thought his eyes were on me for a full ten minutes. Ruth flashed a smile in the temple lobby. "Hey, guess what?" she said. "We're not supposed to talk to you for forty-eight hours."

It didn't bother me. I was so angry and frightened that I preferred to be left alone. There was too much sarcasm inside. Too many questions needed answers. If I became involved in a conversation the wrong thing might come out. It was good for me to have time to think things through and develop a plan of action.

When my punishment ended, Archie ordered me to the Jim Jones house. I can't tell you the fear I experienced. That week another "disciplinary beating" took place at the San Francisco temple. To my fertile teenage mind the stories of blisters and blood were very real.

As it turned out Jones only wanted me to take one of his daughter's friends to a dance. It should have been a treat—a chance to rub shoulders with outsiders. But I feared I was being tested. The evening was nothing special.

When we got back to the Jones house a strange thing occurred. My date and I were alone. No one was at home waiting for us. The church service was still going strong. My date unlocked the door to the house and told me to wait. I slipped inside, waiting in a darkened house for ten minutes. Nothing happened. There was only darkness and silence.

My eyes began to adjust to the room. I could have snooped around, I thought. No one would have even known. I might have seen some of the notes they always passed to Jim Jones. Maybe I could have found some incriminating document? We'd all been to the Jones house on one errand or another but someone was always around at those times. Now the place was wide open for a search. Of course, they wouldn't just leave things lying in the open, I thought. The most important things would be in his office. Or maybe in his bedroom. The temptation to sneak upstairs to check was great. I had never seen the bedroom of a god.

I should find out where my date is, I thought. Maybe I should telephone the church and tell them I'm back? I could just explain I'm at the Jones house. Walking into the kitchen gave me confidence. I touched the telephone and then decided to look around just for a few seconds before calling. I snooped in a few cabinets and drawers. I opened the refrigerator and the room was momentarily filled with light. The freezer was full of steaks.

In a few minutes I had walked easily through the various downstairs rooms in the house. Soon I was back by the front door, still waiting. I could have made it up to the bedroom and back by now, I thought, glancing one more time at the stairway. Then I made my decision. I could hear someone approaching the house and still get back down the stairs in time. I practiced an innocent look, some mask I could pull over my face if I were caught on the stairway. Slowly I started up, crawling on all fours to distribute my weight and avoid noise.

The stairs squeaked anyway. I reached the top landing, worked my way down the hall and checked out the rooms. A little glow came from the windows from security lights outside. I stood for a moment outside Jim Jones's room. My heart began to beat like a bass drum. It suddenly occurred to me that I was being tested. I thought, I'm being watched. There's a tape recorder—there's a hidden alarm which I've already triggered.

The lights from an automobile flashed across the hallway, causing shadows to dance and jump. I raced down the hall and stumbled down the stairway. My own noise added to my fear. One thing was for sure, if anyone else was hiding in the house, they now knew about me. I waited for some time. Nothing happened. It had only been a passing car.

Once more I worked my way up to the Jones bedroom. The door squeaked as I opened it. Suddenly a light came on downstairs. I could see the glow coming up the hall. Jim Jones? I didn't know. My head began to pound. I stepped into the bedroom. There were two orange crates on either side of the bed exactly as we had been told. I stood behind the door listening to footsteps on the stairway then down the hall. Another light came on in an upstairs bedroom. How long could I remain where I was without being discovered?

The figure retreated back downstairs. I moved into the hallway and waited, listening carefully. Whoever it was, they were busy in the kitchen. I could delay no longer. More people would be arriving. I moved quickly down the stairs. A woman stepped out of the kitchen.

"I'm Phil Kerns," I smiled. "I was one of the escorts to the dance."

She gave me an icy stare. I walked out of the house, feeling her penetrating suspicion like daggers in my back.

My high school instructor's advice proved much more productive than my "Rockford Files"-type detective work. When the heat on me began to let up, I planned a journey to Mendocino County Courthouse.

Everything went off without a hitch that day. I talked to the tax recorders and eventually found a person who was anxious to show me around. "It is a school assignment," I explained. They seemed delighted to find a young person showing such interest.

"They're all public records," my friend explained. "Anyone can see them."

Among other things, I learned that the official incorporators of People's Temple were Jim Jones, his wife Marceline, and Archie Ijames. What troubled me most was that Jim Jones, Archie Ijames, and Jack Beam all owned their own houses.

That clinched it for me. My mother was typical of the little people who gave everything they had to the temple. Watches, wedding rings—my mother would not have thought of owning her own home. Every title was to be transferred to the People's Temple. Then why did the very incorporators and leaders hold title to their own homes?

I listened more carefully to Archie Ijames's telephone conversations, trying to pick up every piece of information I could. One day at the dinner table I casually dropped a question. "Archie, do you own your own house?"

Archie almost dropped his fork. I had cornered him and he knew it. Mama Ijames scowled. I returned her look with an innocent expression. "I was only asking a question. Sorry." Thereafter, Archie kept his eye on me. He once caught me listening to him on the phone. I protested innocence but thereafter he and his telephone retreated to the bedroom for important calls.

The climax finally came. We were in the middle of our letter-writing campaign. Fifteen of us were crowded into the upstairs rooms of a two-story house in Ukiah. I was tired. There was no time for homework. We spent hours stuffing envelopes. I began to grow weary of the conversation of my co-workers. "Oh, did you see that tonight? Jim Jones has a gift. He's so wonderful." We worked till 3:00 A.M.

After another day of school, we were back to work. I began to become aware of what was going on. He's using us, I thought. I looked around the room and saw all the other people. These people are crazy. We're all mad, and I'm the most stupid of all. I've talked my sister Jeanette into this thing. I felt guilty and angry. I looked into the eyes of my co-workers. "Oh, no," I muttered. "We're all crazy!"

I left the workroom and ran downstairs. One of the guards stopped me. "Where are you going? You can't leave here."

"I'm sick," I protested. "I'm sick!"

He laughed. "No sir! You're not sick. Not yet. You've got more work to do. Now get back up there."

I knew in a moment what I was going to do. I was going to leave. Now—at this very instant—without spending another day in this nut house. Jeanette was living at Tim Stoen's house nearby. I wanted to talk to her, warn her, but there was no time. That would only make trouble for her.

I ran. As fast as I could go —I ran across the parking lot. Through the arms of a guard at the gate and out into the evening. For a few minutes I hid in the park nearby and watched them. It took a moment for them to organize a posse. No one could just leave. We were always checked. They had to know where we were and who we talked to. The cause was too precious. There were too many enemies. Two cars screeched out of the parking lot to find me.

Let them race around, I thought. They don't have dogs so they won't find me easily on foot. I lay on my belly in the park when it suddenly dawned on me what I had done. If they found me I would go through hell, worse than the beatings, the public ridicule, their kangaroo court on stage. I lay in the semi-darkness, my heart pounding.

When the commotion subsided, I worked my way to the edge of the park and across the street to a fire station. I had to get out of view so I walked into the open garage. A man eyed me suspiciously.

"Do you know anything about Jim Jones?" I asked. I was so frightened that I could hear my own heartbeat.

"He's crazy," the fireman said. He looked me up and down and chuckled.

"What makes you think so?"

"That guy is possessed," he answered. "If anyone has ever been possessed by a demon, that man has."

I was amazed. I had never heard anyone speak so openly against Jones.

"Aren't you afraid of him?"

He cursed and spat. "I'm not afraid." Then he smiled at me. "You're the one they're looking for, ain't ya?"

I didn't answer.

"It's all right," he said. "As far as I'm concerned you ain't ever been here."

"Oh, thanks." I didn't know if I could trust him. It might be courage. It might be bravado.

"He's socking money right and left," the fireman continued. "He's taking title to people's homes. I have a friend who became a member. The guy's insane."

I found myself reacting to his comments. I wanted to defend Jones. I gave this man a hard look and then took off.

Moving unseen through Ukiah was no easy task. I jumped from one doorway to the next, really expecting to be seen and caught. I wasn't. I reached the highway, darted across and sat hidden in a little drain ditch. Should I try to hitch a ride? Should I wait? I decided if I waited too long the letter-writing campaign work might end. The highway would be full of Jones's people.

I jumped up, my heart racing. I stuck out my thumb. It was dusk and very hard for a person in a car to see. The first one that passed stopped and pulled over. I was sure it was one of Jones's people.

The car didn't move. Nobody got out. That seemed like the Jones style, cocky. "Come on, Kerns!" I imagined someone in the car saying. "You aren't going anywhere."

Maybe I should run, I thought. Would they chase me? Still there was the chance that this was a complete stranger. I had to take the risk.

"Pretty late to be hitchhiking," he said. Just one old man driving home. I could not believe my luck. "I can get you up the road aways," he said. "Not very far."

"That's fine," I said. Then, as an afterthought, "You couldn't drop me off on the other side of the city so I could get a little head start?" He grunted without answering my question but when the time came he deposited me right where I asked.

Now I would be safe. But the paranoia still lingered. You cannot imagine the terror I felt. Every approaching car made me tremble. I actually felt good about a car as it went on down the road. "Another person in the world who does not belong to the Jones family. Hurray! Jones lives in a very small

83

world. Hurray for freedom. Hurray for America! Hurray for the FBI! Come and get me!"

Soon there were only headlights with no prospects of a ride. I was hungry. I had no money. Still my only fear was Jones.

Eventually a car slowed down. It was an old Volkswagen. It rattled by and came to a stop. I approached it carefully. It was not a car I recognized. This could be my trip to San Francisco I thought—or this could be them.

As I approached, a voice from the Volkswagen spoke very softly. "Get in, Phil." I felt a chill run down my spine. It was all over. They had me again.

They returned me to People's Temple. There was complete silence during the trip. I felt like a kid with an "F" on his report card. But what could they do? Why was there such fear? How could they keep me?

At the temple I telephoned Archie Ijames. I had never heard him become so angry. "Phil, where have you been?" I didn't know what to say.

Archie drove immediately to the temple. "Get in," he ordered, but his voice sounded kind. "Phil, it's okay," he said. "What's wrong?"

"I'm sorry," I answered him. "I've been so tired. We've been stuffing envelopes all week."

"Well, Philip," he smiled. "We all have to do things we don't want to do."

"Why? Why?" I was suddenly angry. The whole thing was so absurd. People can't order you around like robots. They could beat me. So what? They could kill me. So what!

"You don't ask why, Phil," Archie said. "Now come on home. Mama's got something to eat."

Loyalty was the key word in the Jones family. But it should have been blackmail. That's why some male members of the inner circle eventually allowed photographs to be taken of them committing sexual acts with Jones. That's why they signed statements claiming to have molested their own children. That's why in some cases they signed over powers of attorney. And eventually that's why communards were not allowed to leave Jonestown, Guyana, unless a husband, wife or child were left behind as a hostage. Loyalty, once given, could never be taken back.

Though much of this corruption will be discussed in later chapters, the seeds existed in 1970. I was suspect now. Everything I did was watched. Mama Ijames became fearsome. She wanted a complete report on everything that happened in my life.

To get out of the house I visited some People's Temple members down the street. They usually had a pot of spaghetti on and I played the guitar, entertaining their little girl.

One day the father pounced on me. "You've been making advances."

"What?" I didn't understand him.

"You've been molesting my daughter!" he screamed.

85

"No!" I shouted back. "Ask her; she'll tell you."

"Yes!" the mother shouted. "Get out, Phil! We don't want to call the police."

I fled. They are sick, I thought. She is only a little girl. They are sick. They must know it isn't true. I was confused. I was hurt. For a long time I wept.

A couple of days later, I was approached at the church. "Listen, Phil," one of Jones's men said. "This thing about the little girl. Those parents are probably wrong. I know you, Phil; you're a good kid. As long as you stay put, Father Jim will take care of you. He can keep them in line, but if you run off it will look like you're guilty."

I saw it in a moment. Blackmail? They had to be kidding. Then and there I decided I would get away. If I had to steal and lie and plan for months. If I had to turn my back on my mother, I would still get away. They would not keep me. I was angry.

The Christopher Lewis affair also took place about that time. Lewis was a big black man, a drug addict, a pimp. I don't know why he took a liking to me. We visited a lot. I sort of became his little brother.

Lewis had sent his wife to bed with a man and then robbed him, people in the cult had said. Jones hired a big attorney and got Lewis off the hook. "Look at this man," Jones would say. "He used to be a drug addict; now he babysits with kids."

They always put Lewis with children. It looked like a great contrast to see this big, violent ex-con taking care of little children. "See how Jim Jones can change your life," they would say.

Sometimes Lewis took me into San Francisco with him. His wife would get out, walk the streets and bring back money. Lewis was soon right back on drugs. One rainy night we sat in the car and talked while his wife hustled.

"Do you think Jones would blackmail someone?" I asked.

He looked at me hard. I told him the story of the little girl. Lewis laughed.

"Listen," he said. "I was a lot better off pimping and on drugs than being with Jones."

"But he got you out," I said. "Everybody thinks he got you out of jail."

He scowled. "Jones can get you out and Jones can get you in."

"What do you mean?" I asked.

"You just got to be a good soldier," he said. "You gotta do what you're told. That's what I mean. Jones has got San Francisco locked up. He can get what he wants."

"Do you think I could just leave?" I asked. "What could they do to me?"

Lewis just stared out at the rain. "I don't know," he said. "They couldn't do nothin' to you." Then he paused. "But I can't leave."

I didn't ask him why. I knew he wouldn't answer.

A few years later Jones would become furious with a young man named Rory Hight. Christopher Lewis would murder him with dozens of witnesses looking on. Jones's lawyers would go to work. Within a short time Lewis would be free, walking the streets again.

On December 10, 1977, Lewis was chased down a San Francisco street by two gunmen. To no avail, he banged on doors and windows for help. He was shot to death. Lewis was wrong. There was one way out of the family. Eventually, more than 900 people would take that same way out.

By working at the high school lunchroom I had started to build a little savings for my escape. Occasionally, on little excursions to town, I stopped by an army surplus store. I eyed a $15.00 backpack. When I get $30.00 I'll take off, I decided. That was enough for the backpack and a ticket for Santa Rosa with some change left over.

One night I bought the pack. I hid it in the bushes a short distance from Archie's house. Over a period of days, I shifted my valuables and necessities to my little cache. Then the time came for the break.

Archie's son was home. It was a special occasion. He was an airplane pilot and a hero at People's Temple. A hometown boy who made good. His presence changed the mood of the house. Mama Ijames was happy and proud. No one seemed to notice me come or go. It was a perfect time.

"Jim Jones will be one of the most renowned and well-known men in the world," Archie's son told me.

"You're sure?" I asked. The whole table scowled at me.

"Someday the whole world will be talking about him," he said.

Archie's son was a great singer. One of the best I had ever heard. We all bragged on him a little. Mama Ijames looked at me and smiled for the first time in months.

That night I slipped out of the house and packed the final time.

The following day was graduation. I grabbed my diploma and fled. I didn't wait for the ceremony. I didn't parade across the platform. I had a bus schedule to keep.

When I arrived home, Mama Ijames smiled big. I showed her my diploma. She was happy, slapping me on the back and throwing out congratulations. "Well, I can't take the day off to celebrate," I said. "Got to get busy for Father Jim."

"Yeah, you get busy," she said.

I ran out, grabbed my backpack and took off. I ran so hard my side ached. I climbed up to the highway in broad daylight and stuck out my thumb. O God, I thought—not Jim Jones but the real God—help me. I stood there shaking like a leaf, praying, holding out my thumb.

As each car would pass I would mumble, "Mister, please, mister. This is an emergency, help me."

Finally, an old jalopy stopped. I froze. It looked like a hippie at the wheel. I ran to the car and jumped in.

"What are you doing? Running away from home?"

he asked.

I laughed. Was it written on my face? When would he identify himself and tell me he was taking me back?

"No, I'm just bumming around," I said.

He dropped me off at the Ukiah bus station.

Ukiah is a small town filled with members of the family. I saw Larry Leyton crossing the street, headed my way. I assumed he had spotted me. He walked right by, not seeing me in a group of people. Carl, one of the tall ushers, walked by. I raced to the ticket counter.

"Your bus is leaving."

"Hurry, please!" I said. "I've got to make that bus."

There was paperwork she insisted on doing. I raced out to the bus to plead with the driver. His door was closed. I banged. He opened.

"Please. I've got to make this bus or I'm in big, big trouble," I begged. "She's writing my ticket now."

"I've got to go kid," he said sternly. His chest was filled with pins and awards. He looked like the type who would keep his schedule.

I raced back in, grabbed my ticket, and ran back out. He opened the door.

"Sorry," I said.

"Take a seat, son," he said angrily.

I sat back and sighed deeply. The glass windows were tinted. We rode through the city looking out on the world, but the world could not see us. There were family members all over the Ukiah streets. I saw Tim Stoen walking down the courthouse steps.

You beat them, I told myself. You made it. I smiled as the bus pulled out on the highway. Then I put my head back and relaxed. I cannot explain the relief I felt. In minutes I was asleep. It was the best sleep I had experienced in years.

When I awakened, I saw a man sitting next to me. He looked like he had been waiting for me to get up.

"Where are you headed?" he asked.

"Santa Rosa," I said. Was he a member of the family? A spy?

"You have family up there?" he asked.

"No."

"Well, why are you going there?" he persisted.

My suspicion really heightened. Still, I had never seen his face around the temple. I decided to talk to him about Jones to gauge his reaction. The more I talked, the more convinced I was that this man was an outsider. I could trust him. He wasn't going to turn me in.

"This Jones is an incredible man," he said.

I felt a compulsion to tell him about all of the so-called miracles, prophecies and healings which I thought were fake and some that were mysterious. Here I was running for my life and even then I found myself bragging about Jones.

"Maybe he is the Christ," the man said.

I couldn't believe it. "It's too much for me," I said. "But some of the people in Ukiah think so."

"You know," he continued. "All my life, I've been looking for the Christ. Not some invisible character—but a person."

Is everybody in the world crazy, I thought. Is this man serious? "Well, I'm not sure," I said. "This man could be, but I'm afraid it's too much for me to handle."

During the rest of the trip, he pumped me with questions. I told him all about the family. Even some of the things that had bothered me: He was the first outsider I had really talked to in months.

"You know what?" he said. "This guy could be the Christ. Do you believe in reincarnation?"

I paused. "I don't know." Then I asked him, "What are you going to do?"

He laughed at himself. "Well, I was on my way to Texas," he explained. "But I'm going to go back to Ukiah and have a look. I have to be certain. I have to know. I'll never forgive myself if I don't check it out."

I was so dumbfounded that I suspected he was putting me on. I followed him into the Santa Rosa bus station and stayed with him, talking things over. He exchanged his ticket and filled out a refund voucher for the balance.

"Thanks, Phil." He stuck out his hand. We clasped out hands together. "And now where are you going?"

"I don't know," I said. I only had two dollars in my pocket.

"I really hope you know what you're doing," he said. "You're sure you want to run away from them?"

By the look on his face I knew he would go back. I felt badly. Years later, I would begin an investigation of Jones. I would begin to collect information on the rumors of murder and sexual abuse. I would go back to try to get my mother and sister out. One night, while sitting in the balcony of the new People's Temple in Southern California, I would be approached by an usher—the same man I had met on the bus.

Rev. Jim Jones

People's Temple, San Francisco, California

Rep. Leo Ryan who, along with several newsmen, was murdered in Guyana while investigating Jim Jones and his cult.

Bodies lie strewn around a vat containing a drink laced with cyanide at the Jonestown commune of the People's Temple. (UPI)

Some of the hundreds of people who killed themselves at the command of Jim Jones. (UPI)

The body of Jim Jones lies shot to death among the bodies of his followers. (UPI)

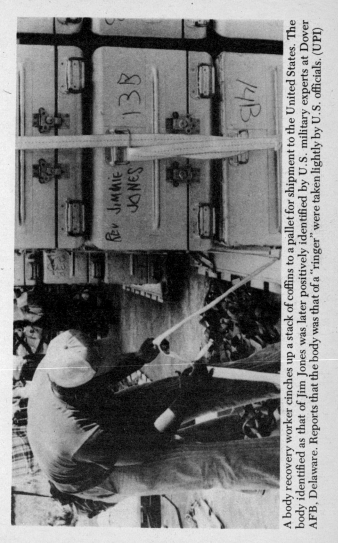

A body recovery worker cinches up a stack of coffins to a pallet for shipment to the United States. The body identified as that of Jim Jones was later positively identified by U.S. military experts at Dover AFB, Delaware. Reports that the body was that of a "ringer" were taken lightly by U.S. officials. (UPI)

Captain Davidson of the Guyana defense force examines some of the weapons found at the People's Temple mission building. (UPI)

Bodies of some of the over 900 persons who died in the mass murder-suicide in Jonestown are placed in metal caskets by members of the U.S. military personnel. (UPI)

A member of the U.S. military body recovery unit sent to Guyana walks past rows of metal caskets containing bodies of victims of the mass murder-suicide at Jonestown. (UPI)

A C-130 U.S. Air Force airplane which was used to ferry dead bodies from Jonestown, Guyana, to Dover AFB, Delaware. (UPI)

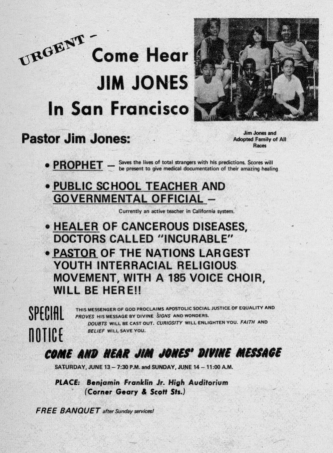

*URGENT —*

# Come Hear
# JIM JONES
# In San Francisco

Jim Jones and
Adopted Family of All
Races

## Pastor Jim Jones:

- **PROPHET** — Saves the lives of total strangers with his predictions. Scores will be present to give medical documentation of their amazing healing

- **PUBLIC SCHOOL TEACHER** AND **GOVERNMENTAL OFFICIAL** —
  Currently an active teacher in California system.

- **HEALER** OF CANCEROUS DISEASES, DOCTORS CALLED "INCURABLE"

- **PASTOR** OF THE NATIONS LARGEST YOUTH INTERRACIAL RELIGIOUS MOVEMENT, WITH A 185 VOICE CHOIR, WILL BE HERE!!

**SPECIAL NOTICE**

THIS MESSENGER OF GOD PROCLAIMS APOSTOLIC SOCIAL JUSTICE OF EQUALITY AND *PROVES* HIS MESSAGE BY DIVINE *SIGNS* AND WONDERS.
*DOUBTS* WILL BE CAST OUT. *CURIOSITY* WILL ENLIGHTEN YOU. *FAITH* AND *BELIEF* WILL SAVE YOU.

### COME AND HEAR JIM JONES' DIVINE MESSAGE

SATURDAY, JUNE 13 — 7:30 P.M. and SUNDAY, JUNE 14 — 11:00 A.M.

**PLACE: Benjamin Franklin Jr. High Auditorium**
**(Corner Geary & Scott Sts.)**

*FREE BANQUET after Sunday services!*

A flyer announcing one of Jim Jones's meetings.

*Thank you for your contribution to*

**PEOPLE'S TEMPLE CHRISTIAN CHURCH**
**P.O. Box 214**
**Redwood Valley, Calif. 95470**

*This contribution will help to aid our Temple Welfare Ministry, which gives aid and assistance to hundreds of people each week.*

This accompanied a receipt for contributions to the People's Temple.

| | | | |
|---|---|---|---|
| 6SALEM | OR | 3648798 | |
| 6SALEM | OR | 3648798 | |
| 80RCHARDS | WA | 3892570 | 206 |
| 8BERKELEY | CA | 5481773 | 415 |
| 8WASHINGTON | DC | 3244614 | 202 |
| 8WASHINGTON | DC | 4564009 | 202 |
| 8RESEDA | CA | 3457219 | 213 |
| 8WASHINGTON | DC | 6329226 | 202 |
| 8WASHINGTON | DC | 6329226 | 202 |
| 8SAN FRAN | CA | 5391173 | 415 |
| 8SAN FRAN | CA | 5391173 | 415 |
| 8BERKELEY | CA | 5848177 | 415 |
| 8WASHINGTON | DC | 6329226 | 202 |
| 8WASHINGTON | DC | 3244615 | 202 |
| 9SAN FRAN | CA | 5526077 | 415 |
| 9SAN FRAN | CA | 5863077 | 415 |
| 9BERKELEY | CA | 6264995 | 415 |
| 9WASHINGTON | DC | 5848177 | 415 |
| 9WASHINGTON | DC | 3244614 | 202 |
| 9WASHINGTON | DC | 3244614 | 202 |

| | | | |
|---|---|---|---|
| 1119 | SAN FRAN | CA | 415 6264995 |
| 1119 | SAN FRAN | CA | 415 6264995 |
| 1119 | BERKELEY | CA | 415 5391173 |
| 1119 | WASHINGTON | CA | 415 5848177 |
| 1119 | WASHINGTON | DC | 202 3244614 |
| 1119 | WASHINGTON | DC | 202 6324120 |
| 1119 | WASHINGTON | DC | 202 6866300 |
| 1119 | WASHINGTON | DC | 202 6864200 |
| 1119 | WASHINGTON WEST | DC | 205 2943460 |
| 1119 | KEY WEST | FL | 302 6866420 |
| 1119 | WASHINGTON | DC | 205 2943805 |
| 1119 | FRINGTON | CA | 202 6293807 |
| 1119 | RIVERSIDE | CA | 714 6894995 |
| 1119 | SAN FRAN | CA | 415 6264995 |
| 1119 | WASHINGTON | DC | 202 6293380 |
| 1119 | WASHINGTON | DC | 202 3244614 |
| 1119 | SAN FRAN | CA | 415 5391173 |
| 1119 | SAN FRAN | CA | 415 5391173 |

PAGE 5 (CONTD 760 6102 NOV) — PAGE 6 (CONTD 760 6102 NOV)

| City | State | Number | Time | Number |
|---|---|---|---|---|
| SAN FRAN | CA | 4155522155 | 1120 | |
| KEY WEST | FL | 3052944618 | 1120 | |
| COMPTON | CA | 2136342705 | 1120 | |
| WASHINGTON | DC | 2026329380 | 1120 | |
| WASHINGTON | DC | 2024561414 | 1120 | |
| SAN FRAN | CA | 4155529380 | 1120 | |
| WASHINGTON | DC | 2023242805 | 1120 | |
| BERKELEY | CA | 4158481773 | 1120 | |
| SAN FRAN | CA | 4155522155 | 1120 | |
| WASHINGTON | DC | 2024561414 | 1120 | |
| SAN FRAN | CA | 2136342705 | 1120 | |
| WASHINGTON | DC | 2136553911 | 1120 | |
| COMPTON | CA | 2026329380 | 1120 | |
| BERKELEY | CA | 4158481773 | 1120 | |
| NEW YORK | NY | 2127512600 | 1120 | |
| PLAINFIELD | NJ | 2017540745 | 1120 | |
| NEW YORK | NY | 2127512600 | 1120 | |
| SAN FRAN | CA | 4156264995 | 1120 | |

| Number | State | City | Time | Number |
|---|---|---|---|---|
| 4157772424 | CA | SAN FRAN | 1120 | |
| 2139743611 | CA | LOSANGELES | 1120 | |
| 2132748878 | CA | BEVERLYHLS | 1120 | |
| 2026329380 | DC | WASHINGTON | 1120 | |
| 2026326611 | DC | WASHINGTON | 1120 | |
| 2026326995 | CA | SAN FRAN | 1120 | |
| 4155626499 | CA | SAN FRAN | 1120 | |
| 4159811849 | CA | SAN FRAN | 1120 | |
| 4154217616 | CA | SAN FRAN | 1120 | |
| 4155421761 | CA | SAN FRAN | 1120 | |
| 4155626499 | CA | SAN FRAN | 1120 | |
| 4154217616 | CA | BERKELEY | 1120 | |
| 4158421773 | CA | WASHINGTON | 1120 | |
| 4154217616 | DC | MERRILL | 1120 | |
| 2026326610 | OR | COMPTON | 1120 | |
| 7985393 | CA | SALEM | 1120 | |
| 2136342705I | OR | ORCHARDS | 1120 | |
| 3990907I | WA | | | |
| 2068925701I | | | | |

Copies of Phil Kerns's phone bills for November, 1978. Note calls made to Washington before news of the mass murder-suicides reached the U.S.

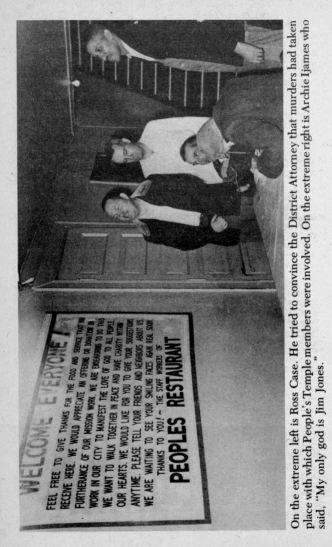

On the extreme left is Ross Case. He tried to convince the District Attorney that murders had taken place with which People's Temple members were involved. On the extreme right is Archie Ijames who said, "My only god is Jim Jones."

The author's mother in a photograph taken some years ago. She
was among those who perished at Jonestown.

From left, the author's sisters, Carol Ann and Jeanette, and his wife, Vicki. Carol Ann is wearing a necklace with a picture of Jim Jones. She was among those who died at Jonestown.

# six

## *My Investigation Begins*

The hold of Jim Jones on my life lingered for years. I married. I joined the army. I led a normal life with the bizarre nightmare of People's Temple far behind me. Still, there were moments when it all came back. Mostly I was troubled about my mother and sister who were still there. What was going on? If I went back to get them would they listen to me?

An event occurred in my life which must be included in this story. Without understanding this, you would not be able to appreciate why I continued to pursue my mother and sisters. The uncovering of evidence of murder, the threats on my life which followed—not even these could deter me. Not because of bravery. Not because I was a fool, though there may be a point to that argument. It was a positive motivation. I had no ax to grind. I had good news for my mother and my sisters and Archie Ijames and for Jim Jones too.

When I received my honorable discharge I learned that Ruth and Jeanette had left the Jones family. Ruth was living with thirty people in a big mansion in northern California. Oh, no, I thought, another cult. My wife knew how my mother and sister concerned me. She knew I wouldn't rest until I got them out, so she suggested we talk things over with Ruth. Maybe we could come up with a plan. Vicki and I, and our new baby, followed her instructions and wound our way up to the big Carlotta Mansion. The place was well lighted. There was a giant wooden cross in front. It looked ridiculous and fanatical.

The people inside were happy; Ruth hugged me, her face glowing. We sat and talked for hours. She was especially kind to Vicki and soon my wife was at ease. From the other room came the sounds of a folk guitar. There was singing. It was a joyous song.

Eventually we joined them. This was the Jesus movement, then sweeping the country. I was amazed. There was no stage, no demagogue, no fear. There was an incredible group consciousness; there was unity, but it was unity through joy, not fear. And it was voluntary.

Someone stood and talked about Jesus. I cannot describe my feelings except to say that there was an opposite sensation to that of the Jones meetings.

This was spontaneous and it shook me. All of the mysteries of the sacraments, all of the teachings of ancient Christianity came back.

I'll tell you what troubled me. I had shaken off religion, and emotionalism, and anything that bordered on the mystical and spiritual. Now, however, my heart was responding but based upon my previous experiences, alarm bells were going off.

We were planning to spend the night at a motel but Ruth stopped us. "Oh, please stay right here."

Others chimed in, giving us a welcome. "No use wasting your money."

Our room was clean and there were fresh flowers on a dresser. Over the bed was a poster "Jesus Christ is Lord." Do they mean Jim Jones, I thought. No, there was a different kind of Jesus here. Vicki and I slept soundly.

At the breakfast table everyone gave audible praise to God—not to a man on a stage. I experienced great sensations of joy and I could feel love. This was not some superficial love, or some love ideal. This was real. The distinction was clear. In the Jones family we always talked about how happy we were, as if to reinforce something we doubted, but wanted to be true. At that breakfast table we were tasting—really tasting—happiness.

Jim Jones is a fraud, I thought. He has to be. I know it! I imagined I was feeling the power of an eternal God and I was ready to listen.

There was a Bible study. Ruth talked to me about

the death of Jesus. Then one of Ruth's friends pulled out the Bible again and started reading the Gospel of John. Here it was, the very Word of God. The book I had seen Jones throw to the floor and spit on and curse violently. I strained for every word. It was soothing, just like an ointment taking away the pain and hurt. No one lectured or interpreted or explained. We just listened to the Bible.

I've heard some reviews of the Britisher who quotes the Gospel of Mark on the Broadway stage. They say it is stunning and moving. One would actually have to read through one of the Gospels aloud to understand what began to happen to me at that kitchen table.

I felt foolish. How could I have missed such an obvious, ancient, and available book like the Bible? Why had I never read it before? Sometimes I felt guilt, then some illustration or powerful words of Jesus would rush in on me and wash the guilt away. At times we began to cry, all of us at the table. The Bible reader would blink his eyes and struggle on. It was all so wonderful, so pure, but was it practical?

"Yes," they said. "On your own it is not. No amount of discipline can make it work. You should have learned that at People's Temple. Their ideals are good but motive and means are just as important as the goal. The key is that the Spirit of God will help you strive for this ideal."

It was all so wonderful. I wanted to crawl up in the Bible and hide between the words. But Jesus was saying, "Go." His last message on earth commands us, "Go." I had to get my mother and my sister and Archie Ijames and all the people I loved out of that place. I had to tell Jim Jones that Jesus is Lord.

When I announced these intentions Ruth laughed. "First you need to make Jesus your own Lord," she said.

"You need Christ," someone else said.

I was spooked. Old fears of exploitation and group pressure returned. I knew a psychologist would say, "Yes, religions are all the same. Jesus was someone just like Jones. This sensation you feel is autosuggestion or mass hypnosis. Jones or Jesus, you are just the kind of person who needs a crutch."

Should I throw away my chance to taste one of the most enduring and beautiful spiritual experiences in the world, just because of the ridicule of an imaginary psychologist? How do we know his evaluation isn't some kind of academic mass hypnosis?

The warmth of the Gospel of John lingered. I could see Jesus, not strutting around in His glory, not planning promotional schemes with His disciples, but just sitting by the Sea of Galilee cooking some fish on the beach. I was out in the water fishing like Peter, and Jesus was simply telling me to throw my net on the other side. It was a story we had just read.

"You have fear, don't you, Phil?" one at the table asked.

"I've been living with fears all my life," I answered. "It's a part of the Jones culture to be afraid."

He started praying. "Jesus, show Phil, take his fear away."

"Jesus, take my fears away," I said and then I repeated what they had been saying last night. "Jesus is the Lord, the Son of God!" Just saying it brought indescribable joy, and such peace. How could I have avoided God so long? It seemed so stupid to think that in all of time and space that man was the greatest intelligence, that there was nothing bigger. Even in the limited confines of earth there is the great diversity between a human and an ant. To say we are alone, rulers of an empty universe struck me as limited and stupid.

Now, I began to realize something. This faith in God, this peace, was what I had looked for in Jim Jones. It was what the man on the bus was searching for. I had found it here in this ancient book. What happened in a Jones meeting could not compare with the joy and peace that came to me here. It overflowed. We all laughed and cried and embraced. They got out the guitar and the flute and we sang.

They read the Scripture; I will never forget it. I grabbed it when they were finished to see if it were true. It was read from one of the new Bible versions. "I know very well how foolish it sounds to those who are lost, when they hear that Jesus died to save them. But we who are saved recognize this message as the very power of God. For God says, 'I will destroy all human plans of salvation no matter how wise they seem to be, and ignore the best ideas of men, even the most brilliant of them.' For God in his wisdom saw to it that the world would never find God through human brilliance, and then he stepped in and saved all those who believed his message, which the world calls foolish and silly." (1 Cor. 1:18, 19, 21 TLB)

We lived for one year in the Carlotta Mansion. The day we left, they crowded around us. We wept and embraced. As we drove away, Vicki and I comforted each other. With tears running down our faces, we reminded each other that God's love is not a location or a guitar or a flute. God's love is eternal and once we have tasted it we can never escape its embrace. Now, we had to go back to the People's Temple and share this truth with others. I thought of myself as a missionary to a foreign country, maybe even a missionary to another planet.

Jim Jones had been doing a little missionary work himself. Besides the temples in Redwood Valley and San Francisco, he had opened a branch in Southern California. When our attempts to get into People's Temple in the north were rebuffed, we journeyed to the Los Angeles area hoping to infiltrate the family there.

The Southern California temple was a big, ugly

block building in downtown Los Angeles. Jones's buses were lined up outside. Good, we thought. The people from Ukiah are probably down here. Jones had a way of busing the same audience to different auditoriums, giving the illusion of several mass congregations.

We walked in through the front doors past a lobby full of merchandise. There were pictures of Jones and trinkets and jewelry on sale. By that time Jones was telling his audience, "You don't need to have sex with each other. Have sex with my picture!"

There were security guards everywhere. They wore little arm patches. I saw them stopping people. I grabbed our little baby from Vicki's arms and headed with confidence toward a balcony stairway.

There was another set of doors ahead of me. I could hear the voice of Jim Jones echoing. He was preaching equality. I felt sick when I heard the sound of his voice. Go ahead, I told myself; you go in there and you let him holler at you, just keep your mind on Christ.

The guard stopped me. "Don't you know me?" I said. "I'm Penney duPont's son. Come on." They apologized and explained that no one was allowed in unless they were a member or guest. They frisked us and let us pass through.

The auditorium was hot. It was filled with sweaty bodies fanning themselves. We sat in the balcony and felt the stares of the entire audience. It was strange. The whole audience turned to look but

Jones went on as if there were no interruption.

Jones was walking up and down the aisles, wearing a long robe, his jet-black hair and dark sunglasses, his visible trademarks. "Oh, the spirit loves you," he said. I suddenly realized he always had referred to the spirit, not God, not the Almighty, not the Holy Spirit, only the spirit. What spirit, I wondered.

"I need to touch you," he said. The crowd went crazy.

Archie Ijames grabbed the microphone and coached the audience. "Now don't be selfish. Think of others too."

People grabbed him and touched his body all over. "Oh, Jim; oh, Father Jim!" Chills went down my spine.

Jones whirled and spotted a woman in the audience. "Oh, mama, I know you've had arthritis all your life! Now put your hands up. Bend over; reach out. Run up there on the platform."

The black woman ran; Jim chased her, clapping and whooping it up. The audience shouted and clapped. They all believed she was healed. The audience started shouting in rhythm, "Yes! Yes! Yes!"

Jones pointed at a man. "I know you've been deaf in one ear," he spoke sternly. "Isn't that right?"

"Yes, father," he answered. I chuckled. The old man was twice Jim Jones's age.

"Now!" Jim shouted. "Ear? Start hearing."

The audience went crazy. They crowded into the aisle with ushers holding them back. "Stop it! Stop it!" Jones shouted. "Hold it down! Stop the band!" He turned back to a man in the audience. "Your name is Bernard." He feigned a trance, "Bernard, Bernard. Oh, spirit, what is it?" Then suddenly he shouted, "Bernard Hudson!"

"Yes," the man nodded vigorously.

"I know you've been in pain all your life!"

"Yes."

The man was fairly new. I could just tell by the naive expression on his face. Jones is really going to work him over, I thought.

"You went to a doctor," and then Jones called names, dates, exact information. "The doctor said you have a tumor. Is that right?"

"Yes," his eyes were wide open in astonishment.

"Here's what I want you to do." He turned to the crowd. "Everybody, the pain is here." He pointed to the man. "Stretch your hands this direction. Okay, here's the pain."

Jones touched him in the stomach. "Now!" he shouted. Then calmly, "Okay, you go with the nurses in there and get rid of that tumor!"

The man ran to a room on the side, paused by the door and turned back. "Thank you! Thank you! Thank you!"

The man's sudden enthusiasm struck the audience funny. They all laughed as if to say, "See, we've been trying to tell you newcomers about

Jones. It's all true. He knows everything."

Jim smiled humbly. "That's all right," and waved him on. Another miracle, so what? Jim Jones had much more power and virtue than that.

"Isn't it wonderful to be with father?" Archie Ijames said. "Isn't it wonderful to be a part of this socialist dream?"

Jones's magic show had improved in the short years since I left. The messengers arrived like little bees whispering in his ear. The number of so-called miracles had increased dramatically. The show was faster, with such astonishing scenes that I could not figure out how they were staged and faked. Could Jones have some parapsychological gift, I wondered? In the context of my new Christian faith, I wondered if he could possess some satanic powers.

Though many wished that the miracles were all true, I soon learned that Jones had only become more professional at staging his show. Homes were now burglarized regularly in order to obtain information to back up his "prescient gifts." Even the members' mail was tampered with.

That very night the nurses returned with what was supposed to be the man's tumor. This was a much more realistic-looking one than the animal parts that had been used at Redwood Valley. The crowd cheered. Jones grabbed the microphone.

"I want you all to know that I was Marx! I was Lenin! I was Jesus Christ and I am here again tonight!" The crowd went crazy and after basking in the cheers for a long time he motioned for quiet. There was an obedient hush.

Jones's voice pierced the silence. "I am the second coming of Christ!" The audience went into a frenzy.

There, in the middle of the cheering crowd, I spotted my mother. She turned and saw me. For just seconds we gazed at each other over the gyrating throng. Finally, she waved and rushed to the balcony. I met her at the steps.

"Oh, honey, I'm so glad you are here," she said. Then she eyed me suspiciously. "Where's the wife you told me about in your letter?"

We walked to my seat in the balcony. She talked to Vicki and took the baby and cuddled it and laughed. "Oh, he's so cute," she said.

Carol was happy to see me but I sensed that she approached me with caution. Jones had taught us always to be suspicious of anybody who defected from the family. Such traitors couldn't be trusted. I looked at Carol, now a beautiful young lady, and wondered how brainwashed she had become.

We sat for another hour. I was restless, anxious to talk to them both, foolish enough to think I could shake their faith in Jones.

There were some dramatic moments in the service. "Get that S.O.B. out of here. That man back there is with the FBI! You get out of here—now!" he screamed. The man, either a helpless visitor or a Jones plant, ran out with people cursing him.

"Mom, I haven't seen you in so long," I said.

"Could we go outside and talk?"

She frowned, but then agreed. We left the baby with Vicki and went outside. As soon as we left the building, I unloaded all the pent-up things I had wanted to tell her.

"Mom, I'm a Christian," I said. "I believe in Jesus."

"Don't give me that s___!" She spat on the ground. "I've been through that. Those preachers never did anything for me. Jim Jones is the only one who ever did anything for me. Jim Jones doesn't talk about Jesus—he is Jesus!"

"But, mom, it's not the preachers," I insisted. "Preachers are just men. Jones is just a man. He will fail you. All men eventually fail. There is a real Jesus—a real person—not some imitation."

"Don't give me that!" she screamed and then stalked off.

"Carol," I pleaded, turning to my little sister, "I'm your brother, at least listen to me."

"Jim Jones is the only god I've ever known," she said.

"But, Carol, there is a real one—a real God," I protested. "A God so big that Jim Jones looks cheap beside him. And Carol you can talk to God and He loves you."

Her eyes darted back and forth nervously. "And the Jesus Jim talks about—Carol, there really is a Jesus," I said. "Jones is not Jesus. There is a real one. He doesn't need all this phony stuff!"

Jack Beam came out and saw us together. Mother

had probably sent him. He took one look and went back into the temple lobby. A moment later he returned, this time with four others, including Larry Leyton.

"Phil," Beam said, "is everything okay? How have you been?"

"Oh, fine," I answered calmly. "We're just visiting. I haven't seen my sister."

"Well, I really think we ought to go back in," Beam said. "Jim has a lot of important things to say."

"Okay," I promised, "we'll be right in. We are just visiting a minute."

"I really think Carol needs to come in," he insisted politely.

I was angry. This was all so ridiculous. "Look, this is a free country," I said. "Let her alone. Let Carol decide."

He motioned with his hand. She looked into my face with wonder as if I were a member of another species, then she walked away.

I was crushed. I walked to the fence and looked up into the night. Oh, God, God! Where is your power? Is there a way to break these terrible chains around my sister?

Vicki and I returned to the meetings from time to time. We were careful to avoid attention. I thought if I laid low I might be able to pick up information that could expose the whole thing.

One night Jones pointed his finger and a woman fell over dead. It was a chilling performance. "I see you!" he screamed, pointing to the back of the auditorium. "Your name is Janice Smith and you've been selfish all your life. You've taken and taken but you never give. You have been here three times and never once given an offering. I've had a vision," Jones paused. "Oh, no. You're dead, ma'am. I'm sorry. You're dead!"

A woman stood up, walked out and fell over in the lobby. In the confusion, I slipped outside quickly. An usher from the back announced, "She's dead!" The audience gasped.

An ambulance arrived within minutes. I watched furtively from the side of the building while they lifted her into the ambulance.

I raced to my car and roared down the street just in time to pick up the siren. They went around a few blocks and then stopped at the curb. The supposedly-dead woman was now sitting upright, talking nonchalantly to the usher. I drove on by and went home.

At the time, I was working in a machine shop in Southern California. Whenever possible, I pushed the events of the People's Temple away from my thoughts but never for long. I felt a burden, a responsibility, for Carol and mother.

On one occasion, filled with anger and frustration, I went to the temple determined to come away with evidence. From previous visits I had located the hub of activity. It was a series of rooms directly behind the stage. I had attempted to reach the area from the outside. Everything was locked. Once I had seen Jack Beam roaming around a room in the back. He was packing a pistol.

Now I had an idea. There may be an access to the back stage through the basement. Perhaps it would be less secure.

That night I wandered confidently into the basement. There were people preparing cups of Kool-Aid and making cookies. I initiated a conversation with a woman and soon my confidence jumped contagiously from one to the next. They were all reassured.

I moved to the back stairway and slowly worked my way up. I could hear voices in the room just above me. There were shadows on the ceiling. From my position I could not be seen either by the woman in the basement or the persons just above me. At the top of the stairs a guard was posted. Should I try to bluff my way further or should I wait to see if he leaves?

As it happened, I did not have to make that decision. The guard was called away. I ascended the stairs and was immediately confronted with a maze of little rooms. I darted down a narrow hallway, avoiding the voices around me.

There it was. The "inner sanctum"—Jim Jones's room. I recognized his clothing. On a little bed were hand-written notes. There were dozens of them. They contained names and information for his miracle performance. On the other side of the wall I could hear his voice.

I stood frozen, surprised by my find. I could reach out and pick up a handful of notes and show my mother. See, he is a fraud. Look at the handwriting on this one and here is another. Whose handwriting is this? They were all different. They came from different messengers, Jones's stage assistants. Come on, mother, admit it, I would tell her, it's all phony. My mother, who owns no home, who gives 75 percent of her income to People's Temple, who works all hours of the night to help the cause, would probably have said, "So what? Jim Jones is the only one who ever did anything for me."

There were footsteps down the hallway. I jumped away from the bed, stood near the doorway and looked out—right into the face of Archie Ijames. "Hey," I said cheerfully. "I've been looking for you."

"Phil!" His face registered alarm. "How did you get back here? You can't be here. What are you doing?" He looked around as if he were worried for me.

Just beyond two sliding doors I caught a glimpse of a folding table. It was piled high with little mountains of money. A group stood around the table, counting it all and putting it in neat stacks.

"You're not supposed to be here, Phil," Ijames warned.

I left through the quickest exit which happened to lead me right into the front of the auditorium. Jones was down one of the aisles in the middle of his act.

He stopped, spotted me, and stared hard and mean. His ushers picked up on this signal and raced down the aisle toward me. I left the temple, with the ushers rushing me along.

When I got to the car I slumped over the steering wheel. Fraud was not enough. Even if I proved it, the cause was greater than faked clairvoyance. My mother and sister seemed lost to this madman.

After her Christian experience, my sister Ruth had not talked much about Jones. It was a depressing chapter of her life, one she wanted to leave closed. Now she opened up to me, trying to help me find the flaw that might shake our mother and sister free.

Ruth's own exit from People's Temple had been dramatic. She had boldly announced her departure, calling Jones a phony and a liar. They all followed her right up to the gate—including Jones himself—screaming and cursing at her. Others had begged her to stay, but no one stopped her as she walked right out. Those in the People's Temple with lots of self-confidence could get away with a scene like that. There weren't too many. People's Temple had a way of stealing your self-confidence.

Most importantly, Ruth provided me with the names of persons in the family whose faith had been shaken. These were people who had been ready to leave at the time she bolted. Maybe I could play on their doubts and get them to open up?

That is exactly what happened and the news was terrifying. All kind of allegations were floating around. I was told Jones was going far beyond burglarizing homes. There was talk of sexual abuse and murder. Stories about Maxine Harpe's suicide were coming back. In "family legend" there were now six mysterious deaths. Rumors linked them to Jones. There was great fear.

I was so agitated and troubled. Could this be true? I was concerned for all of them, not just my own mother and sister. How could such idealistic, self-disciplined people be involved in something so sinister?

One morning I awakened and found myself dismissing all these murder theories. They seemed ridiculous in the light of day. The whole bizarre Jones world seemed impossible. No doubt many of my fears were born during my impressionable teenage years. What was real; what was fantasy? These were reasonable people.

I journeyed to Ukiah to confront Archie Ijames. I loved Archie. He had been like a father to me. We had worked together and wept together. These were reasonable people, I thought.

Papa Ijames was pleased to see me. The sincerity in his eyes swept away all the horrible stories. "Phil, how have you been?"

"Can I talk to you?" I asked.

"Phil, I'm really busy," he said. "We've got a lot to do."

"Well, I've driven a long way. Please," I said.

"What is it?" Archie squinted at me.

"Listen," I began awkwardly. "I've heard you used to be a Christian. You were a lay minister in a church. You must know the difference between Jim Jones and God!"

Archie stared at me with a dumbfounded look on his face. He was transfixed.

"Listen, please," I begged. "I've found Jesus, the real Jesus. I want you to know God loves you. Archie, He still loves you."

Archie paused calmly; then he erupted like a volcano. "Don't give me that s__!" The exact words my mother had used. "You get the hell out of here! Don't bother me!"

I had never seen this gentle man explode like this. He had often put his arm around me to encourage me and tell me I was his son. The anger literally poured from him.

"Get him away from me!" he shouted. "S__! S__!"

It was an astonishing scene. I felt like a priest holding a crucifix in the face of a vampire. He could not stand to hear about it. I left.

The next day I sat in my car several blocks from the People's Temple. My contact came rushing up, opened the door and jumped in. He sat for a moment, catching his breath. "It's getting bad," he said. "Jones's sex life is really getting kinky. One of my friends heard him say he can go to bed with any of the girls when they reach eighteen."

I didn't hear the rest of his information. I sat at the steering wheel, paralyzed by grief and sick to my stomach. I panicked, trying to figure out if Carol were now seventeen or eighteen. Oh, God, how could you allow this? I was in agony. The Jones balloon had to break. If it took leaving my job and moving to San Francisco I would do it. If I couldn't convince my own mother, maybe I could convince the authorities, the district attorney, the California State Justice Department.

I was in for a big surprise. The nightmare of Jim Jones was very real and his people were everywhere.

# seven

## *Eight Mysterious Deaths*

My inquiries into the so-called "Jones family murders" began soon after our move to San Francisco. I drove to the temple one night for a rendezvous with an old friend of Ruth's. As we had arranged, I parked my car down the street and waited for his arrival.

A young black man suddenly jumped into the car. It was as if he had materialized from thin air. "You Ruth's brother?" he asked.

"I'm Phil Kerns," I said, a little frightened. "Yes, I'm her brother."

The youth opened up to me. There were things he had been waiting to tell someone for months. He told how violent the beatings were becoming. He told of a young man who was commanded to take down his pants and expose himself in front of the whole congregation. This was a punishment. "And there have been murders," he said.

"You can prove that?" I asked, sitting up quickly.

"Yes," he promised.

"You realize," I said, "Jones has power. He can cover up almost anything. But if we can prove just one murder we can get this whole thing shut down!"

He shook his head vigorously. "It can be done!"

We only talked for a few minutes but I could see he was obviously frightened. He warned that we should set up a meeting for which he could obtain a better alibi, something reasonable which could let him get away long enough to tell what he knew.

I met him again the following month. His information was very sketchy but it was a beginning. He suggested that one of Ruth's old girl friends would know more. I planned to meet her the very next night but I was in for an unexpected occurrence.

My mother showed up instead. She was intensely angry!

"Mom, what's wrong?" I asked innocently. I was not sure if she had just stumbled onto me accidentally or someone had spotted me and alerted her.

"What are you doing here?" she snapped. "You're a traitor!"

"Mom," I pleaded.

"Look at this car!" She was shocked. I was driving a cheap little import but to her it was bourgeoisie and too materialistic. "What are you doing running around in this fancy sports car?"

"Mom, it's okay," I said. Then I grabbed her and held her. For only seconds there was a slight response. Then as if acting on a stage, she pulled away mechanically. She sneered at me, her beautiful face contorted in an ugly expression. She turned and walked off. I would never see my mother again.

My three years in the Bay area were the most frustrating of my life. The Jones family deteriorated rapidly. The violence and sex stories increased. Still, there was nothing to prove murder. I drove hundreds of miles, racking up thousands of dollars worth of phone calls. I didn't have much to show for all the time and money except rumors and the kind of evidence that works perfectly on a TV murder mystery but holds no water in a courtroom.

There were eight mysterious deaths related to the People's Temple. I had organized some information about them, and I was probing for every piece of first-hand information I could get.

1. *Maxine Harpe.* On March 28, 1970, she was found swinging from a noose. According to the coroner's report, she had stood on a trunk, tied a heavy cord around the rafters of her garage, wound the cord around her neck and jumped. A lot of people in the Jones family were suspicious of the so-called suicide. Now I learned we had not been the only ones. Carolyn Pickering, reporter for the

*Indianapolis Star*, had been asking questions. The *San Francisco Examiner* ran an article. But the newspapers had come up with nothing substantial.

What I learned from friends was sickening. Maxine had begun dating Jim Randolph, one of Jim Jones's henchmen. Jones was jealous of their relationship. My friend overheard him say, "Maxine needs to have her attention focused on me, not Jim Randolph!" He wanted Maxine's total loyalty.

According to another friend, Jim Jones had told Randolph to "destroy the relationship." Maxine was tearful and upset. Jones, furious because she mourned her lover, had taunted her. "Why don't you just kill yourself? Get it over with!" This statement was also overheard by my second source. Another friend said Jones had sneered at her and told her that "at least Judas had the guts to kill himself."

Finally, in his bitterness and wrath, Jones had prophesied her suicide before a small gathering. Maxine herself was present. That was the week in which I had seen her troubled and frightened. No wonder! Jones's prophecies, including automobile accidents, were always fulfilled. In fact, on one occasion he announced to the audience, "The prophet is responsible to make the prophecy come true."

The night of her death Maxine did a strange thing for one who was contemplating suicide. But it was a perfectly understandable thing for one who was fearing murder. Maxine had asked if she could take several children home with her. The house was full of children. Tom Ijames, James Moore, Danny Harpe, Kathy Harpe and another little sister. The oldest was ten. At 1:30 A.M. Tom Ijames wandered out into the garage and found Maxine hanging from the rafters. The little children then called the People's Temple. Maxine's children and babies watched as temple members removed a Jim Jones healing cloth from her body. The house was ransacked and anything which could identify the temple was removed.

There is a final bizarre note to this tragedy. Years later, after the 1978 mass suicides, I contacted a former member of the People's Temple council. She is now a Christian and was troubled by the fact that she had introduced Maxine to the cult. She had been present at a meeting shortly after Maxine's supposed suicide. It was a closed meeting, with approximately sixty in attendance. Jim Randolph was brought before the group whereupon Jones began to rant and rave at him. "You know you did it!" According to the eyewitness, Randolph did not break, even after Jones verbally worked him over.

2. *Emily Leonard.* She was an elderly white woman who lived in South San Francisco. She had turned her property over to the temple and then a storm began. Relatives convinced her she had made a mistake. Emily and her relatives secured legal help and planned to go to court. She died that same week.

Shortly thereafter, a Mr. Wade Medlock and his

wife were confronted at the temple in Los Angeles. Jeannie Myrtle told me that they were asked to sign over their property to the church or die. Jones had allegedly said, "One person attempted to get her property back and I killed her."

3. *Azrie Hood.* She was an elderly woman who wrote Birdy Maribelle and Ross Case, two Ukiah friends who were not members of the temple. Azrie was a member of the People's Temple in Marshall, Texas, who wanted out. She warned that her telephone had been tapped. Birdy, Ross and Brenda Ganatos were planning to give her money to fly from the Shreveport, Louisiana, airport to San Francisco where they would pick her up.

The old woman declined their offer, and in a possibly fatal mistake, used her telephone to tell her friends she would not bother them for money. She would just wait for her Social Security check which was to come the first of the month. Azrie Hood disappeared within hours of that phone call. She has never been found.

4. *Leo Blair.* He owned a little grocery store in Redwood Valley. Allegedly, Jim Jones wanted it. Blair said, "No!" Suddenly, he found himself in a gigantic mess. Two young temple girls claimed he had molested them. There was a lot of hatred and venom coming forth from temple members. I remembered Leo. He had impressed me as being a

kind man. I'm sure he was stunned by the organized harassment which suddenly descended on him. Jones never did get his property, but Blair didn't have it much longer either. He committed suicide.

5. *Curtis Buckley.* The story was that Buckley had overdosed. Three things about this bothered my friends. One, the fact that Buckley wasn't known to have ever taken drugs. Two, he had been observed carrying a large amount of cash into the temple on the day he died. Three, the complaints of Janet Schuller, his stepmother. She declared his medical records had been tampered with. The Buckley case bothered me even more than the others, but it was the one with the least evidence to indicate foul play.

I was troubled by Buckley's friends who were very intense and seemed very convinced that he had been murdered. On paper that means nothing but hearing it from those who knew him was quite a different story.

6. *John Head.* On September 27, 1975, two People's Temple members visited John. He was escorted to a bank where he withdrew some money. He then turned it over to the temple. The next day Head told his mother he was going to live with the Jones people. On October 19, he reportedly committed suicide. Allegedly, he jumped from a building. Many family members felt he had been pushed.

The coroner's report was confusing. Mrs. Head, the boy's mother, was suspicious. Various pages reported different accounts of his death—that John had jumped from a bridge, from a three-story warehouse, and another page indicated he had simply died at 212 North Vignes Street. The report stated that there were no scars on his body, but his mother wondered how they could miss a giant scar on his leg. This remained from a motorcycle accident and had required three hundred stitches.

Mrs. Head wanted an inquiry. The Los Angeles Coroner's Department refused.

7. *Truth Hart*. Truth was an elderly black lady, living at the Maribelle Rest Home. Truth had died in very mysterious circumstances. According to one eyewitness, it was murder.

Jones's very idealistic operation began quite generously in its ministry to the elderly. As Jones's own ego soared and his personality deteriorated, he began his exploitation of the older members. Those on Social Security or disability were required to turn checks over to the temple. In return, the cult began providing them with less and less.

Jean Foley was typical of those who would try to hold some of their checks back. Sometimes she would be locked in her room and her blankets would be taken away.

Not all the rest homes deteriorated to the level of a concentration camp. Birdy Maribelle ran a clean ship. She had been a member of People's Temple for some time but when some of the residents of her own home were exploited, she quit. She objected openly—a brave thing to do in the little city of Ukiah where most offices, including that of the sheriff, were thought to be controlled by the Jones people.

When a Mendocino County newspaper investigated the situation, Birdy talked openly to them. She reported that a Harvey Lawson was forcibly removed from her rest home. He was hauled out, tied up in a sheet, kicking and flailing at his kidnappers. "Jones wants us to bring him dead or alive," People's Temple members had told her.

The Truth Hart incident began in 1974. Hart started to speak out in the services of the temple and this irritated Jim Jones. There were reports that she had been complaining behind his back.

Numerous witnesses remember a public prophecy that had been given by Jim Jones. He was in his full acting character, his omnipotent posture, when impulsively he stated, "That woman will die soon!"

Shortly thereafter, the People's Temple organized a bus trip to the East Coast. Jones told Birdy Maribelle to pack her bags. Birdy wouldn't leave her responsibilities at the rest home. Jim arranged for the temple people to take over and then encouraged others to talk Birdy into the trip.

Birdy finally did leave and Mary Black took over. According to witnesses, Mary Black was also known as Mary Love, a former worker for Father Divine, the black preacher who claimed to be God.

The rumors began to pick up. According to "family legend," Truth Hart was pinched and tormented by Black. She was put in a bathtub, then pulled out. According to eyewitnesses, a pill was given to Hart. She was told to drink a glass of water. She then laid on her bed and died.

One of the witnesses was Janie Brown who said, "Look, she's already dead!" Another witness was Ella May Hoskins.

The coroner arrived and, according to Hoskins, without any examination, the doctor simply asked, "How did she die?"

Mary Black allegedly said, "Heart attack."

Birdy Maribelle began to suspect she had been lured away from Ukiah so they could get to Hart. While back East she made some remark of concern about Hart to Jim Jones. Jones said, "It's better this way, Birdy."

The two eyewitnesses in Ukiah were crusty old women who were not easily intimidated at first. They suspected murder. Janie Brown stood in a public meeting to declare, "I don't care what anybody says about Truth Hart; I know what really happened!"

Days after this public announcement—on January 29, 1975—Janie Brown also died. Her death was not reported to the coroner and the line on her death certificate contains no signature of the coroner's name.

Reverend Case, a local pastor, was troubled. He obtained testimonies from all involved and presented it to the police, the sheriff's department, and the district attorney. He got nowhere. The assistant district attorney was People's Temple member, Tim Stoen.

An intensified harassment of Case now began, including threats of death. Attempts to see the minister lose his job as a public school teacher failed. A temple member went to the principal claiming to have had homosexual acts with Case and my own mother, Penney duPont, testified that she had personally witnessed it. In the Case situation, the man's personal integrity proved even greater than all the temple resources. He survived but his inquiry into the death of Truth Hart had failed.

There is one postscript to the Hart story. The other witness, Ella May Hoskins, is still living. After the mass suicides, Doug Wead, the co-author of this book, made contact with Ella May. The woman was frightened and unwilling to talk. A second attempt proved successful, however. Members of the rest home had seen the author on the PTL Club television program. Ella May opened up, confirming the whole story.

"Was this just a family legend that grew with time?" Wead asked. "Or were the residents of the home immediately suspicious of the death?"

Ella May Hoskins answered clearly, "We all

believed it was murder—immediately!"

8. *Bob Houston*. The most famous of the temple's mysterious deaths had this intellectual and sensitive man as the victim. On orders from Jones he had divorced his wife and married one who was chosen for him. Jones ordered him to move into a slum apartment to take care of twenty-four children. He and his wife maintained fifty-hour work weeks, turning over 10,000 dollars a year to the temple. They were true humanitarians and socialists.

Bob's problem was his colorful intellect. He could not keep it under wraps and the threatened Jones retaliated. Houston was beaten for every minor infraction. These so-called disciplinary actions took place in front of the whole congregation with Houston's children looking on in terror. A larger man would beat on him until Jones would call a halt. His widow told the *San Francisco Examiner* that Jones laughed during one of these scenes.

Eventually, Joyce Shaw, his new wife, left the temple. Bob Houston suddenly became the literal whipping boy. Everybody jumped on him. The pressure increased. Ever the intellectual and philosopher, he thought there was some hidden reason or special kindness Jones was trying to communicate through these actions.

Meanwhile, Bob's parents longed to see their granddaughters. The visits were "controlled" and the elder Houstons were told that if they wanted to give Pat and Judy gifts they had to give similar gifts to all the other children in the commune. Bob loved his daughters but displayed no public favoritism and accepted his socialist duty when he was ordered to be separated from them.

As the brutal storm rose, Houston seemed to remain unaware of the strangeness of events. He knew he had special talents and took on two jobs to help the family. In the nights he served as a switchman in the Southern Pacific rail yards. One of my sources spoke of meeting him there. "Bob was a meticulous man. He always wore his gloves to keep his hands clean. He never took his gloves off while working. But when I approached him he took off a glove and reached out with a clean hand to shake."

On October 2, 1976, Bob Houston, brilliant, sensitive—yet blind to the anger his socialist purity caused—was found dead. His body was mangled on the tracks. His glove was found neatly on a coupler nearby. Everyone was asking the question. Had Bob been approached by someone before his death? Someone he recognized? Someone he naively greeted with a gloveless handshake?

Pat and Judy? Their grandparents longed for them. They were whisked to New York for a vacation. Actual destination? Guyana. Jones was establishing a model socialist commune in South America. The older Houstons had more tragedy before them.

These eight mysterious deaths demanded some kind of inquiry. As sketchy as my information was, it was still enough to prompt some kind of investigation in normal circumstances. But these were not normal times or normal people.

Jones had friends everywhere. In 1975, he delivered a block of votes to help elect San Francisco mayor, George Moscone. The thankful Moscone made Jones chairman of the housing authority. District Attorney Joe Freitas and the *San Francisco Chronicle* city editor were also friends. In fact, Freitas was described by members of the family as a "close, close friend," probably to frighten and discourage anyone from going to him with charges.

I felt like an ant climbing a growing mountain. I was getting somewhere, all right, but the mountain had grown more than I had climbed. Jones's massive letter-writing campaign extolled the virtues of his social work. This brought commendations from America's great Democratic Party leaders, including Hubert Humphrey and Henry Jackson. Gov. Jerry Brown visited the People's Temple and, from the pulpit I had built, praised Jim Jones. While on the campaign trail, Rosalynn Carter dined with Jones at the Stanford Court Hotel.

Maybe Jones was right. Maybe he was going to be a world leader. Maybe he would take over the whole state, the whole country! Maybe I'd end up in a People's Temple concentration camp.

The whole thing was destroying me. Poring over

the gruesome facts of these mysterious deaths had not been very healthy. My personal career was suffering. Vicki was frightened. After four months of soul-searching I sighed in desperation and gave up. I resigned myself to the fact that I had temporarily lost my mother and sister. I could not let that knowledge destroy me and my little family. We packed up and moved to Oregon to start a new life together. As far as I was concerned, Jim Jones was behind me.

# eight

## *Absolute Power—*
## *Total Depravity*

Freed from the fears surrounding Jones's immediate presence, I could take time to reflect on my experience. The more I thought about it, the more angry and guilty I became. I could not abandon my mother and sister. Given the same set of circumstances, they would have lovingly and stubbornly pursued me until I was free.

In the libraries of Portland, Oregon, I began to put together an interesting profile of Jim Jones. Then, one night while watching a Bell Telephone commercial, I decided to call some old friends in San Francisco. My telephone investigation proved frustrating at first but eventually I built up quite a network of sources. I found people were willing to talk from within the confines of an untapped telephone booth especially if the voice on the other end of the line was in Portland, Oregon. Ruth and Jeanette provided names of old friends both in and out of the temple.

The picture that emerged was one of a spellbinding megalomaniac who maintained a public image of social justice and sacrificial humanism but who subjugated his followers to absolute obedience through sexual intimidation, threats of violence, mob pressure, and constant indoctrination.

His public representation was still so good that politicians bent over backwards to obtain his favor. His People's Temple following in California was considered the largest Protestant church in the state, and it carried sizable political clout.

Jones's list of direct and indirect political connections grew rapidly during the mid-1970s. California Gov. Jerry Brown considered appointing Jones to the state Board of Corrections, and the governor was among several prominent political leaders present at a People's Temple commemorative ceremony honoring the birth of Martin Luther King. In 1976, California's then Lt. Gov. Mervyn Dymally visited the new Jonestown commune in South America. The project showed signs of hope.

The high-ranking temple official, Tim Stoen, was a deputy district attorney in Mendocino County, California, and he later became deputy district attorney in San Francisco. The cult maintained temples in both areas under Stoen's jurisdiction. There were accusations that Stoen had used his authority to illegally obtain property for the cult and to cover up temple improprieties.

The religious community, perhaps out of tolerance, appeared to condone Jones's "ministry," or at least that portion of it which was known publicly.

The Disciples of Christ had ordained Jones in 1964, and evidently did not find enough proof to defrock the controversial minister even after aberrations in doctrine began to leak out from behind the walls of People's Temple.

Jones allegedly was affiliated with other denominations along the way, including an independent Pentecostal church. Jones served on the staff of the church in Indianapolis for two years, until the senior pastor sensed the young minister was spiritually unsound. Jones reportedly tried to make inroads into the Indiana Assemblies of God, and brought large groups to their Indianapolis fellowship meetings. The Assemblies carefully steered clear of Jones's activities, however, and declined to recognize his ministry with ordination.

People who knew Jim Jones in his hometown of Lynn, Indiana, saw at least two sides to the youngster's personality. On the one hand, he was compassionate toward stray animals, and often could be seen leading a parade of pets down the street. But others recalled that by the first grade Jimmy's vocabulary had been well-stocked with gutter expletives, and that he had possessed the ability to herd other children about at will, alternately whipping them into line and preaching to them in an old barn. One neighbor observed that the Jones boy would either do a lot of good, or become another Hitler.

Like Hitler and Lenin and George Washington and Jefferson, Jones's father died while he was young. A neighbor who babysat with Jimmy while his mother worked saw to it that the boy attended the local Nazarene church regularly. In high school, Jones was described as reserved, and a roommate at Indiana University, where Jones attended for a time, recalled the young man as being unfriendly and "weird."

After about ten years of intermittent studies at Butler University, Jones obtained a Bachelor of Arts degree in education. He met a nurse in the hospital where he worked part-time. Marceline Baldwin became Jones's first and only wife, a relationship which helped contribute to his public image despite the fact that in the latter days of his reign, Father Jones committed adultery on a near daily basis with scores of People's Temple members, both men and women.

Jones pastored a small Methodist church for a time, but reportedly left when members scorned his prointegration programs. After stints at several other churches, Jones opened the first People's

Temple in Indianapolis in 1955, a multiracial, liberal work complete with a soup kitchen for the poor and hungry. The Joneses eventually adopted eight children of different races. And in 1961, Jones made his first political inroad by accepting an appointment as director of the Indianapolis Human Rights Commission.

In the early 1960s, Jones seemed to become more aware of his uncanny ability to lead people where he wanted them to go. He came under the influence of the obsessed black cultist, Father Divine, and soon adopted many of Divine's doctrines, including an insistence that his followers be fanatically devoted to him alone.

Finances became the center of focus for Jones. He traded in his old Ford for a new black Cadillac, and began making land deals. He began insisting that followers turn over their money and property to him. A People's Temple nursing home, supposedly a paradise of loving care, was revealed to be a crowded, unsanitary prison, with inmates who were forced to attend People's Temple services. The members were warned that if anyone died on the crowded bus rides, they were not to tell about it.

Jones began denouncing the Bible long before I joined the temple. At first he simply denied belief in the Virgin Birth, but later he spoke out against the whole book. He began his little ceremony of spitting on the Bible and using great profanity to curse it. One got the impression that he was jealous of the book.

Long before the Redwood Valley Church began, Jones started to reveal his growing paranoia about a nuclear holocaust. In 1962 he moved from Indiana to Belo Horizonte, Brazil, supposedly one of the safest places in the world. He later visited Guyana, then returned to the States. By this time he was telling people he was Jesus Christ. Later on he would claim to be the reincarnation of Buddha, Lenin, and Father Divine.

Jones staged his first "healings" in Indianapolis before leaving for Brazil. "Cured" members would go to the bathroom and return with a bloody glob which Jones said was the cancer.

Predicting that the end of the world was coming July 15, 1967, Jones led about 100 followers to another nuclear safety zone—Ukiah, California. Though some of these emigrants dropped out as Jones pressed them to recognize him as God, the leader's unexplainable magnetism gathered in new followers and by 1970 Jones claimed People's Temple had 5,000 members.

The Jim Jones who presented himself to news media wearing threadbare suits and worn shoes was quite a different person from the Jones who ruled his "loving" flock with an iron rod. One girl who had accompanied Jones from Indianapolis was punished three times by being belt-whipped. Her infraction: phoning her parent. Jones told her he was God and she should not need anyone or anything else.

A four-year-old boy on a People's Temple camping trip would not eat all his food, so Jones beat him with a belt and told the boy to eat. The child threw up, and the merciless "father" forced him to eat the vomit.

Jones seemed to enjoy supervising beatings. He introduced the infamous four-foot-long "board of education," a heavy paddle used for punishment, about the same time that I was planning my escape. The paddle was used for such criminal acts as smoking or inadvertently offending "dad." One girl was hit seventy-five times with the paddle for embracing an old friend whom Jones thought was a lesbian. After beatings, penitent victims were required to say, "Thank you, father," after which Jones would embrace them, tell them "father loves you," and assure them they were "stronger people now." Such spankings enabled him to trust them.

In 1971, the People's Temple headquarters was moved to San Francisco. It was there, in 1973, that the first suicide drill was held following the defection of eight temple members. Jones told the people present, after giving them cups of wine and ordering them to drink it, that they had just imbibed poison and would be dead in thirty minutes. For the first "loyalty test," Jones cleverly waited till everyone had already drunk the beverage to announce it was poison. In later suicide drills, fanatical followers voluntarily drank the supposedly-lethal liquid, probably figuring "father" would not really consider killing them.

Jones's sexual gluttony became another focal point. The egotistical leader insisted he only had sex with his followers to satisfy their needs. In frequent temple meetings, sometimes lasting till dawn, Jones repeatedly bemoaned his fate as a sex object. The constant bedroom demands of female followers drained him of his powers, he contended. He forced members to say they were homosexuals and lesbians, and that he was the only true heterosexual. Nonetheless, he frequently demanded sexual liaisons with male followers, often using the encounters as psychological blackmail. And despite his professed reluctance as a "sex object," Jones required all the women closest to him to have sex with him regularly.

He presented himself as the "only legitimate object of sexual desire," and although he had temple members beaten for any acts of homosexuality, real or imagined, he himself bragged about homosexual, as well as heterosexual, encounters. The cult leader taught night classes for a time in a local school district in Mendocino County, and students recalled that Jones spent much of the class time discussing his personal sex life and presenting his pet sexual theories. Armed guards accompanied him to the classroom, and Jones would not tolerate extended disagreements with his statements. The impromptu sex lectures came during history and civics classes.

Finances for People's Temple members were

fairly simple: everything went to Jim Jones. Families signed over homes, property, and paychecks to the temple. To raise additional money for the cult, some members occasionally begged on street corners.

Members who did not live in the church had to tithe a minimum of 25 percent of their earnings. Those living on church property gave everything to Jones, who returned to them a two dollar weekly allowance.

In addition to sexual intimidation and financial imprisonment, part of the People's Temple program of control included erosion of the family structure. Children were encouraged to inform on parents and vice versa. Spouses reported on their mate's infractions of temple rules. Parents were commanded to make up written "confessions" of sexual abuse inflicted on their own children. Youngsters recited prepared speeches about their mothers or fathers who did not belong to the temple. On many occasions Jones ordered followers to divorce husbands or wives who would not take his orders, or who refused to willingly hand over the family's money.

Incredibly, very little of this kind of damning information could get to the public. Disenfranchised cult members, fearing for their lives, seldom made a fuss. Those of us who did speak up were invariably met with excuses from government authorities and police: insufficient evidence. Jones's friendly relations with local media and politicians helped squelch unfavorable reports.

From my home in Portland, Oregon, I watched, and waited and prayed.

# nine

## *Jones Has His Pick*

Information which came to me from sources in San Francisco indicated that a South American People's Temple commune was being planned. People were being shipped to Guyana. I slammed down the telephone receiver and rushed into the bedroom of my Portland, Oregon, home.

"I'm going down there to get my mother and sister," I told Vicki as I packed.

She begged and pleaded but there was no stopping me.

"I don't care what it takes," I told her. "I'll go to the police, the district attorney, the newspapers, the TV stations. I'll raise a ruckus. I'll get something going. I turned and looked full into Vicki's face. "If they ship mom and Carol to South America I'll never get them

161

back."

My wife helped me load the car with the boxes of letters and papers and notes I had collected about Jones. She begged me not to go one more time and then kissed me goodbye with a look of fear and loneliness in her eyes.

The Human Freedom Center in Berkeley had been established by ex-Jones family members. Their little brochure reads, "Dedicated to helping people assume personal responsibility for their own lives."

The ex-members at the center lived in fear. One of these, Jeannie Myrtle, had been a part of the Jones inner circle.

I arrived at her house exhausted and curious.

"Come on in," she said. I followed her into the kitchen and sat down to some coffee. On the counter were a couple of guns.

"I'm so glad I'm out," she said excitedly, "but he sent my children to South America." Jeannie was so nervous she couldn't stay seated. "I want you to know, Phil, I'm writing a book. I'm going to expose this mess. Before they sent her away, my own daughter broke into this place trying to get information on us."

"Calm down, Jeannie," I said. "Please, can you help me locate my mother and sister? I've heard about them shipping people to South America. I'm worried. I want to get them out."

"I saw your mother at the church services," Jeannie said.

"Thank God," I said. "Where does she live now?"

Jeannie Myrtle didn't know. "Check with Neva Sly. She was a good friend."

Mr. Myrtle stepped into the kitchen, said hello to me, and began to brew some more coffee. The telephone rang and Jeannie ran into the other room to answer it. I could overhear the conversation for just a few seconds, then she shut the door.

"We're trying to get our kids out," Mr. Myrtle said.

"Can you help me?" I asked. "Ruth and Jeanette are out. I've got to get to Carol and mom."

"We've contacted a private investigator," Myrtle said. "He's going to help us get our children. You can contact the district attorney's office here in San Francisco. They're trying to get something going. There have been charges of poll-tampering, jury-tampering and murder."

"Tell me about the murders," I said while I sat up.

"There's nothing," he said. "It's all just hearsay. No concrete evidence. The poll-tampering has the best chance. Everybody knows Jones can deliver the votes. We're trying to prove that some of these politicians actually purchased them."

Myrtle's hand shook slightly as he held his coffee cup. It was obvious the Myrtles were frightened.

Jeannie returned to the kitchen. "Oh, Phil, it's bad; it's bad!" She was too excited to sit down. "Jones keeps bragging about his sexual capabilities. He tells all the council that he should bless them by having sex

163

with their wives and they all say 'Yes, Jim, yes, Jim.' "

"That's sick, Jeannie."

She went on to describe an instance when Jones used sex as a form of punishment for insubordination.

I looked at her skeptically.

"I was present, Phil!" she shouted at me. "And he's always saying to the men in front of their wives, 'Now I'm the greatest stud here,' and they all say, 'Yes Jim.' He's telling them not to have sex with each other—just his picture. And all girls eighteen or over are his if he chooses—"

"Okay, okay," I stopped her. "I've heard all that garbage."

"A man is beaten until his tormentor is exhausted, then another man will take over and the beating continues. Jim just loves it."

"I've heard, Jeannie. I've heard. Calm down," I said.

"Did you hear about your own mother?"

I grabbed the chair with my hands until my knuckles turned white but I asked very calmly, "What happened?"

"Your mother has been giving Jim a rough time."

"Go on," I urged.

"Jones told a big group, 'I'm tired of this woman and her complaints. Mr. Silvers, you take care of Penney duPont. You have sex with her every night and make her submit to you, and give me a report once a week. Make her submit!' he shouted."

Outwardly I remained calm. Inside, though, I was furious, even hysterical. I gripped the chair tightly, "And Carol?"

"She's fine right now," Jeannie said. "She's one of the most brainwashed in the whole church. She always helped fix the food. Now she's a courier. She's one of Jones's favorites."

It hurt so badly and so deeply that I wanted to get away to be alone but I knew I needed all the information I could get. "Carol's a beautiful woman now, isn't she?"

"Yes, she is, and Phil," Jeannie warned, "Jones has made it clear he has his pick of the women in the church."

"God," I prayed, "Carol hasn't had a chance."

"You've heard about the suicide pact?" she asked.

"Some friends have been telling me," I said. "What does it all mean?"

Jeannie shrugged, "They just had one in the council meeting. Everybody drank the substance; everybody thought it was poison. Grace Stoen went crazy and Jim called her a traitor. He told us it was just a test to see who was truly loyal. Now they're having regular suicide drills with everybody."

Jeannie's flow of information had momentarily stopped. Then she gave one more parting piece of advice, "Phil, if they know you're here looking for your mother and sister, they'll ship them to Guyana."

I nodded, "That's the chance I have to take. If I don't get them out now, they'll end up there anyway some day."

The district attorney's office was in a large building in downtown San Francisco. I had to go through a metal detector, then up an elevator, and into a plush office. They gave me one of the district attorney's investigators.

"They're shipping my mother and sister to Guyana," I told them. "Can you help me? Why can't you do anything about this Jones guy?"

"All right, Mr. Kerns," he said. "You give us all the information you have and then we will see what we can do about your mother and sister."

"Look," I said. "I want them out of that temple. They've been kidnapped."

"First you're going to answer my questions or you get nothing from us," he snapped.

Some other investigators came in. "What do you know about the murders?" one of them asked. I was suspicious—maybe even paranoid.

"I don't have much time," I said. "You guys aren't going to help me. I've got to get moving or I'm going to lose my sister."

The D.A. slammed his fist on the desk. "I don't have much time either, Mr. Kerns! Now you cooperate with us and we'll cooperate with you."

I started to walk out.

"What do you know about the murders, Kerns?"

Now I was getting just a little frightened. The rumors of Jones and the D.A.'s office haunted me. Why were their questions zeroed in on the murders?

Had they found out I had been studying the issue the last few years? Why not questions on poll-tampering, or beatings or real estate fraud?

I told them a little about the Buckley boy and Bob Houston. I shrugged as I talked as if it were all hearsay and third-hand, though some was not.

"Mr. Kerns, you aren't supposed to go around looking for things," the D.A. said. "You aren't an investigator!"

"Good!" I laughed angrily. "You go talk to temple members and see how far you get."

"Where can we contact you, Mr. Kerns?" he asked.

"Look, we made a deal," I answered him. "I told you what I know. What about your part of the bargain? Get my mother back."

"I'm sorry we can't go in," he answered with a smile. "We have to furnish probable cause that a crime is going to be committed. You can't furnish that, so we can't furnish your mother and sister."

"He's trying to ship them to Guyana!" I shouted.

The district attorney smiled. "What do you want me to do about it?"

I stalked down the hall with a man following me. He stood by the elevator but didn't go down with me. I got to the lobby, a little uncertain and confused. The man who had followed me came huffing and puffing down a large nearby corridor. He had evidently taken the stairway. I stepped into the telephone booth and faked a call in order to have time to think.

A TV crew stood nearby. I was frightened. Maybe the district attorney's office was up to something. I walked over to one of the TV newsmen and spilled my whole story. He smiled, quite taken aback, then even broke into laughter. I'm sure he couldn't follow all that I told him but my urgency and fear was communicated realistically enough.

"Listen," he said. "You need an attorney. There's one right downtown here who's the best. His name is Marvin Lewis. If you can get over there you'll be safe."

Okay, I thought. Let's see what they're going to do now. I walked out. The man from upstairs didn't follow me but, outside, an unmarked car with a small antenna on the back pulled up. I walked a half block with the car following slowly.

This can't be, I thought. This is crazy; this can't be, I'm just a young man, I don't know anything. There are important things going on in this city. Why are they following me around? I took off down an alleyway, hearing the squeal of tires behind me. I ran into the back of a store, took my coat off, folded it over my arm and went out onto the front street. Perhaps with different lights and in a crowd they would not spot me, I hoped. One thing was for sure, I was not going to my car and let them get ahold of my license number.

Within seconds, the unmarked car showed up. The car slowed, then stopped at the corner, where another car took over. I walked a few blocks and turned a couple of corners to satisfy myself that it was not all imaginary. Then I became furious. What an insult to my integrity! What a waste of money! How stupid! They should be following Jim Jones.

I walked up to the curb and waved the car to a stop. "Sir, I'm Phil Kerns. Why are you guys following me?" I inquired. "What's your name?"

He laughed and identified himself as a police sergeant. "We aren't following you. We're on duty."

"What's that?" I asked, pointing to the hearing aid he was wearing.

"That's a radio, son," he smiled.

I stalked off, crossed the street and went into a barber shop. "Listen, I don't want a haircut," I said. "But I'll pay if you'll let me stay in here awhile."

The man looked a little worried. I guess my approach was stupid. We talked for a couple of minutes. I explained that someone was following me. He seemed nervous.

I left, walking briefly down the street. Predictably, the unmarked car wheeled around and followed slowly behind. When I reached the corner I saw a bus approaching on the opposite side of the avenue. I waited until it stopped. People were boarding. I raced across into a crowd and boarded the bus. When I got to my seat and looked back, the unmarked car was still cruising slowly up the street. In my banal, repetitious, cops-and-robbers TV vocabulary, I had "given them the slip."

The bus dropped me off miles away. I stood out in the open like bait, just testing to see if anyone was following nearby. Satisfied that I was now free, I caught a bus back into the city, picked up my car, and headed for the office of Marvin Lewis.

Lewis's office was high in a big building. There was a rack of unique pipes on his desk. One wall was covered with awards, newspaper clippings, keys to various cities and the kind of memorabilia that one of the country's greatest lawyers would have.

"Mr. Kerns?" he greeted me kindly.

"I want you to know," I said, "I don't have much money. Really, I have nothing. But I desperately want to get my mother and sister out of the temple."

"I'm aware of the situation," he replied. "Money's not the problem."

"I'll sign an affidavit that she is crazy," I said. "She has threatened to kill my sister Jeanette. Can we get a court order?"

"It's possible," he said, "but very unlikely. At the present time I'm defending the right of some of the Moonie children who are being kidnapped by their parents." He laughed, "This is ironic; you are trying to get your parent out." He paused thoughtfully. "I must decline," he said. "I'd love to, but I feel this might be a conflict for me."

The private detective's office was my next stop. His name was Mazzore. Neva Sly, my mother's old friend, was with him. Mazzore was angry. He blasted me immediately, "We can't have you snooping around, Kerns! You're going to ruin everything. I'm representing everybody who wants to get their relatives out. I've got to call all the shots. I don't want you involved."

"Well, Mr. Mazzore. That's tough," I said. "It's my mother and sister and I am involved!"

He shouted right back in his intimidating style. "I have clients who pay $5,000 for me. I'm charging all of you one dollar apiece."

I calmed down. "You'd only charge me one dollar?"

"That's right, Kerns," he answered.

"Why?"

"Because I want to see it happen," he said indignantly. "I'm trying to get a lot of people out of Guyana and the temple here in San Francisco."

"How many families do you represent?" I asked.

"Several," he said. Then he stormed at me again. "I don't answer your questions. You answer mine!"

I slapped a dollar bill on the desk and told him everything.

"Now go back to Oregon," Mazzore demanded. "Get out of here!"

I drove down to the temple that evening. I found some little black kids and called them into a little circle. "I'm an investigator," I said. I pulled out a little picture of my mother. "I'm looking for this woman."

"I ain't seen her," one said.

"Look, you guys want a job?" I asked.

"Yeah! How much?" they hollered.

"Five bucks apiece," I said.

"Yea! Yea! Okay!" They went crazy.

"And ten bucks to the one who finds her!" I offered.

Those little kids were all over the temple that night. In and out of little rooms they went, reporting back from hour to hour, but they had no luck.

"Sorry, mister," one of the little boys said.

By early morning I had another idea. I ascended the stairs of a slum apartment and found a door with lights coming into the hallway from the transom above. "Are you awake in there?" I shouted.

A black woman answered.

"This is an emergency," I said. "I need another change of clothes. An old coat, rags, anything." She opened the door and scowled angrily. "I'll pay you," I said.

She looked me up and down and then broke into laughter. "Come on in," she said. "It ain't none of my business but it sure sounds dumb!"

I left the apartment looking like a wreck. I bought a bottle of wine, spilled it all over my clothes and staggered down to the People's Temple.

For two hours I sat near the gates, ignoring the jeers of the guards. I was just a wino, but my eyes checked out everybody that came into the outside courtyard. At three in the morning I spotted a kind old black woman, a friend of my mother.

"Hey," I shouted. "Remember me?"

She looked around nervously and then walked to the gate. "Phil, what's happened to you?"

"Please," I begged. "I've come all the way from Oregon. I just want to see my mother. Is she all right?"

"Be quiet," she cautioned. "She's okay. She works at a hospital as a nurse's aide. She was just here yesterday."

"Which hospital?" I asked.

The woman looked around and shrugged, "I don't know."

"What about Carol?" I asked eagerly.

"Look." The black woman smiled sympathetically. "I can't stay. They'll be suspicious."

I reached through the fence and stroked her hand lovingly. "Thank you. Thank you."

The adrenaline started flowing. I was so excited. I raced away to the astonishment of the guards who had thought I was a drunk.

There was a telephone booth at a nearby restaurant. Armed with handfuls of change, I began to call. I contacted every hospital in the city. I talked to nurses and bluffed my way into having a few of them open their personnel offices. "It's life and death! It's life and death!" In most cases, the personnel offices were closed and so I had to call every floor of the hospital to see if the nurses had any records of new personnel. It took hours.

I begged and pleaded. I waited long minutes on

hold. I was cut off dozens of times. My fingers were cold and numb. This will be the call, I'd say to God. I know this will be the call, and then thirty minutes later I would still be dropping dimes into the telephone.

At sunrise, I slumped in the booth, totally exhausted and weeping. Please, God; please, God. Let me find her outside of that fence. Let me talk to her five minutes. Let me hold her one more time.

After a cup of coffee at the restaurant and another pocketful of change, I would hit the telephone booth again. When there were no more phone calls to make I drove to several of the hospitals. I talked my way into the hearts of nurses who would run all over the place trying to find a record with my mother's name on it. After I checked all the hospitals, I tried convalescent centers.

That morning I slept a couple of hours in my car, parked at the back of a gasoline station. When I returned to the Myrtles for more information, Jeannie greeted me furiously. "You blew it! You blew it! They saw you at the People's Temple. You were supposed to have cooperated with the private investigator. Mazzore told you to get out of town!"

"Jeannie," I slumped on her kitchen table. "I just want my mother and sister."

"I've got news for you," she said. "They've got your mother right now in People's Temple and they are going to ship her to Guyana. And that black friend of hers, you just may have cost her her life!"

"God, no!" I begged, holding my head in my hands.

Once more I rushed to the district attorney's office. "They've kidnapped my mother!" I shouted.

"We have no evidence—" he started to say but I interrupted him.

"Listen, they're sending my mother to South America."

He only smiled.

"Someday. Someday," I said, "the whole city of San Francisco is going to know about this. You guys aren't going to get away with this!"

"Mr. Kerns," he shook his head. "You have not helped us with anything. You won't even give us your San Francisco address. We have no way to reach you."

I apologized and sat down. "I'm staying with some friends of my wife," I explained, giving him the address and phone number.

When I returned to the apartment I had one thing in mind—sleep. If I could get four hours or so I would be ready to go.

Vicki's friend stood at the doorway. "Oh, God," she said. Her face was white. "Where have you been, Phil? I just got a call at work. They're going to kill you. They say they're going to kill me. This was just delivered. She handed me a note. The word "kill" was on it.

"The phone's been ringing," she sobbed, "but I'm afraid to answer it. I don't want anything to do with this Jones thing. You promised not to give out my address!"

"I didn't. I didn't," I said. "Not even to the Myrtles or my best friends."

"Well, somebody has been calling the landlady too!" she said.

"God," I prayed. "What's happening? How could they have found out? I only told the district attorney's people." Then I suddenly realized. "When?" I shouted. "When did they start calling?"

"Just now," she answered. "I just got the call at work and ran back here. What are we going to do?"

The telephone rang. I answered it. "Get out of town," the voice said. "We're going to hurt you!" Click.

My face turned white. Vicki's friend rushed over to me. "Phil, what was it? What's wrong? Oh, God. Help us, God!"

"Calm down!" I shouted back at her. She sat down and cried. "That was Jim Jones," I said. "That was his voice. He said to get out of town."

The telephone rang again. Vicki's friend screamed, "No! Don't answer it!"

I picked up the receiver. "Mr. Kerns, if you don't get out of town, your mother is dead." This time it was another voice. "We'll just chop her up into little pieces!"

"Who is this?" I shouted. Click.

I grabbed the death-threat note, put my coat on and ran out the door. Vicki's friend called to me down the hallway, "What am I supposed to do?"

"Get your friends over here to be with you," I said.

When I entered the district attorney's office I went right for the investigator I had talked to previously. "What did you do with my phone number and address!?"

He saw my anger. "Why?"

I slapped the note down in front of him. "I've had a phone call from Jones."

"Can you prove that?" he asked.

"Listen, buddy," I said. "I'm going to go to some little newspaper in Oregon or Washington and I'm going to tell them my whole story. They're not going to believe me but they'll have all the facts and if anything happens to me, or my wife, or my wife's friend, or my mother, or my sister, you're going to look bad! Bad! You're the only person who knew where I was staying and, another thing, a few days ago you guys had me tailed!"

He looked worried and a little concerned. "Listen, Mr. Kerns," he said. "I just laid your information on that secretary's desk over there. It hasn't left this office."

"Well, I may not be able to prove it to anybody else," I said. "But you and I both know that if I'm telling the truth it means you've got some Jones people in this office."

I drove back to my apartment. Vicki's friends were all over the place. "These Jones people are crazy," someone said. I phoned the district attorney's office to get police protection for the apartment. The answer was negative. I telephoned the police. The answer was no.

"Maybe you should move," I told Vicki's friend.

"There's nowhere to go," she said. "What can I do?"

"Well, I'm going to get out of here," I told her. "There's no use endangering you."

I drove to Mazzore's office. The private detective was not surprised by my story. "I already know the People's Temple has plants in the D.A.'s office," he said. "Now get out of town, Mr. Kerns. You're in the way."

There was one more visit I wanted to make. Neva Sly had been my mother's best friend. She was forty-five years old. She had left the family and was hiding in fear. There were security doors in her apartment. After identifying me, she let me in. We embraced.

"Have you seen my mother?" I asked.

"Yes," she said. "I saw her at the hospital. But she won't be going back there."

"Will they send her to Guyana? Is that true, Neva?"

She nodded. "I'm afraid you shouldn't have been snooping around."

I sighed deeply. Was it all over? Was there anything left to do? Anything else I could try?

"Where's your husband?" I asked.

"Oh, he's already in South America," she said. "He's totally brainwashed."

I put my head in my hands. "What are we going to do, Neva?"

"I'm scared to death," she said. "They are dangerous. Watch out, Phil. You know about the suicide pact?"

I nodded.

"Well, they've also got hit squads to mop up all the defectors," Neva said. "My husband is a member of that group. They mean business. And, Phil," she paused, "don't talk to Mazzore any more. You remember the private investigator?"

"What's happened?" I asked.

"Well," she hesitated. "We have some friends at the temple who say he's been in touch with them. He may have double-crossed us."

"Neva," I said as I stood up, "there's nobody, nobody in the whole San Francisco area we can trust. I'm going to Sacramento!"

I felt fantastic as I drove out of the Bay area even though I knew I had failed. My mother and sister were in Jones's hands. The whole nightmare was unbelievable. But when the scenery changed it seemed as if the whole affair were only imaginary.

Maybe Jones was still the good man I first thought he was. "People will try to smear him," Marcie had once told me. I knew Ruth was wrong about the money. Jones did not have to work himself to death.

Something else drove him. Maybe it was love. Maybe I was not followed at all in San Francisco. Maybe the unmarked cars were doing something else. Maybe the district attorney's office was clean. Maybe Mazzore's actions were misunderstood. Maybe the so-called murders were perfectly explainable. Maybe Jeannie Mrytle's accusations were exaggerated. Maybe a trip to Guyana would be a great experience for mom and Carol. Maybe at some Christmas years from now we would all get together and talk about how ridiculous and paranoid we all were.

Then I began to notice a car in my rear-view mirror. I turned and circled back on the freeway two or three times. The car was definitely following me. Inside was a black man. Paranoid or not, that man and that car were real.

There was one last place to try. I stormed into the governor's offices with all the documentation I could carry. They turned me over to one of the governor's aides.

"You know all about the Jim Jones thing?" I asked.

He leaned forward, listening intently to my tale. "We're getting a lot of reports," he admitted.

"You know the governor has been connected to Jones publicly," I said. "He spoke at his church. You know what it looks like? It looks like he's just trying to jump on the bandwagon and pick up votes. Jones can deliver votes."

"Now just a minute," the aide shouted.

"Wait! Wait!" I said. "I know Brown would never, never go along with this stuff I'm telling you. But if I'm telling the truth, it's going to be embarrassing for the governor. All of us, all the relatives and friends, are willing to testify that Brown was ignorant and innocent of all this Jones stuff. He didn't know about it."

"Right," the aide said. "Thank you. Now, what do you want?"

"We want help," I told him. "We want this madman stopped from hauling people off to Guyana. We want an inquiry into this. I want my mother and sister back. Listen, if anything goes wrong it will look bad for the governor. Okay? I like the governor. He's a neat guy but this isn't politics or style—this is life and death and corruption!"

"Hold it! Hold it, Kerns." He stood up. "You get over to the state attorney general's office. I'll make some calls. We're willing to listen to your story."

I spent several hours at the California state attorney gerneral's office. I gave my story to several investigators. They rushed in and out, checking things as we went along. "All right, Mr. Kerns," a woman in the office concluded. "We're going to look into this matter and we can promise you that nothing is going to happen to your mother and sister, nor to you either. Now, you get back to Portland and let us handle this."

I had a California state patrol escort to the Oregon border. When one patrol car pulled off the freeway, another pulled on, passed by and waved at me, smiling. At last, I thought, the California sun was really shining. It felt good. Somebody believed me. Somebody was going to do something. It was my last try, my last hope. God bless Jerry Brown! God bless the State of California! Tears rolled down my cheeks. My lonely years of frustration were over at last. At least that's what I told myself as I coasted home to Portland.

# ten

## *Till Death Do Us Part*

Three things happened in 1977 which catapulted our family rumors into the national news and threatened to blow the Jones story wide open. The first was a *New West* magazine article. Marshall Kilduff, a *San Francisco Chronicle* reporter who had stubbornly pursued the story, was partly responsible for the breakthrough. With that kind of visibility something had to happen.

Other papers began to pick up the investigation. Jones pulled strings, threatened, organized letter-writing campaigns, but he couldn't hold off the press. He fled to Jonestown, Guyana. I got bad news from my sources in San Francisco—mom and Carol were in South America too.

To gain entry into Guyana, Jones had presented

some sixty "letters of recommendation"—most of which were reportedly simple acknowledgments or thank-you letters from prominent Americans including First Lady Rosalynn Carter, Vice President Walter Mondale, the late Senator Hubert Humphrey, San Francisco Mayor George Moscone, and a host of other well-known political figures.

Once in Guyana, Jones apparently used his powers of persuasion to bend the laws of the tightly controlled socialist nation. He somehow built up a vast weapons arsenal, operated forbidden international communications systems, captained at least three ocean-going boats which the government allowed to come and go with little or no checking, and kept hundreds of thousands of dollars in foreign currency at the commune. The government also allowed Jones to use Guyana National Radio airwaves thirty minutes each week to publicize Jonestown's activities. Citizens of Guyana are not normally allowed such privileges.

Jonestown started out as a model socialistic commune. Or so we thought. A dental surgeon writing in the Guyanese *Chronicle* stated he had never seen so many people of different races working together so harmoniously. He praised the work that had resulted in a community with its own school, saw mill, electricity, roads—all carved out of remote jungles.

Reports slowly leaking back made it sound more like a concentration camp. Passports had been confiscated and no one could get out.

Food rations were cut and workdays were increased to eleven hours per day in 120-degree heat. Only Jones's family and favorite cohorts got meat for dinner. Housing arrangements were grim and crowded. Cultists' sexual lives were determined by a special "relationships committee" which had to approve living arrangements between couples. Jones's own sexual forays continued unabated. Beatings became more brutal, and those who attempted to leave the camp without permission were put to work on a chain gang or they were confined for days on end in a coffin-like "punishment box." Troublesome cultists were imprisoned in the camp's "extended care unit," where they were administered drugs until they were reduced to mute, empty-faced automatons. Even children had to endure brutal punishment for minor sins. Especially "bad" youngsters were taken to a camp well and lowered, hands tied, to the bottom. Jonestown enforcers, hiding in the well, would pull the children under the water, release them, then pull them under again. This would be repeated several times, while the terrified youngsters would cry out, "I'm sorry, father; I'm sorry, father."

Jones called nightly meetings that frequently lasted until 3 A.M.. During these sessions he would rave endlessly about all kinds of subjects. When dead tired followers were finally allowed to go to bed, Jones would often sound an alert over the camp loudspeaker system and order his people to the commune pavilion where he would deliver yet another diatribe against an infinite list of Jonestown's "enemies."

A second major event of 1977 was the defection of Tim Stoen. Tim was the former assistant district attorney of Mendocino County. He later became assistant district attorney of San Francisco. Throughout it all, he was a People's Temple legal advisor. Information sheets prepared by Tim Stoen, plucked from the jungles of Guyana at the very moment of the mass suicide, record visiting numerous banks in and out of the United States while conducting temple business. Needless to say he was close to Jones.

Tim left the cult after one of his trips to Jonestown and did not return. Suddenly he and his wife Grace began to openly charge that Jim Jones was holding their child in South America. Jones said the child was his. A San Francisco newspaper reported on what appeared to be an affidavit that was "floating around." It had been signed by Tim Stoen on February 6, 1972, and witnessed by Marceline M. Jones, the cult leader's wife. The affidavit stated that Stoen had entreated "my beloved pastor, Jim Warren Jones, to sire a child by my wife, Grace Lucy Stoen." In the affidavit Stoen explained that he wanted his child to be fathered by the "most compassionate, honest and courageous human being the world contains."

Stoen's lawyer told the newspapers that when Tim signed the affidavit he really was convinced that Jones was the father. Now he knew different. Jones lawyer Charles Garry said (and most family members agreed), "The child is the spitting image of Jim." The battle was on.

The third major event of the year was the murder of Christopher Lewis. He was my black friend, the one who had once told me that if I left the family they couldn't do anything to me—but he could no longer leave. He spoke of being a good soldier. Jones's money and pull had kept Lewis out of prison a long time. Lewis had been useful to the cult for a wide variety of odd jobs. He had hinted about these dark assignments when he had told me he was better off "pimping and being on drugs" than he was working for Jones.

Finally, Lewis was to be sentenced for one of his crimes. Timothy Stoen predicted Lewis was about to tell all and trade information about People's Temple for a lighter sentence.

On December 10, 1977, before Lewis had a chance to answer questions, before his sentencing, he was shot dead. Two men had chased him down a street in Hunters Point, California. Lewis had run onto the front porch at 1447 Palue, banging on the door for help. They would not let him in. His assailants had never been found. This was murder, not suicide, not a confused coroner's report. This was murder. The Jones controversy was simmering.

The People's Temple fought back. Jim Jones began to pull in his numerous IOU's. In spite of signed affidavits of eyewitnesses charging sexual abuse and beatings, in spite of the pleas of concerned relatives, San Francisco District Attorney Joe Freitas said he found "absolutely nothing" that would make him prosecute Jones.

A temple publication mentioned the Chris Lewis murder: "It was inferred that Chris was a hired bodyguard for Jim Jones. That is an outrageous lie! The temple has never hired anyone, and Chris never worked for us in this or any other capacity."

It went on to say, "If the authors of the news article on Chris Lewis concluded that he was a part of us, then a lot of questions should be raised, because the night of his death a threatening phone call came to the temple saying, 'There will be more. Tonight was the first.'

"It was undoubtedly these lies that said he was a temple bodyguard that got him shot," the propaganda said. "We don't believe this was a gangland murder. We believe the conspirators were responsible. There are those who would sacrifice anyone if it served their purpose. We had to talk to some of his friends outside the church to keep them from taking revenge. This murder we will not forget."

This was typical Jones hype. Turn the accusations around. Jones attempted to convince San Francisco that the now growing body of People's Temple defectors were homocidal, jealous criminal elements he had given his life to help but who had now turned on him.

Propanganda hype was no longer enough. Birdy Maribelle, the nursing home manager who knew too much, found the windows of her home smashed in. Kathy Hunter, a former temple member who is now a reporter for a local newspaper, was pinned to the floor of her home by two black assailants who poured liquor down her throat, covered her clothes with whiskey, and then fled into the night. Jones-style terror tactics had begun. Former members who had heard Jones prophesy their deaths now shivered in fear.

In Jonestown, Guyana, gun battles were staged in the jungles and communards were told that the CIA had sent assassination squads to wipe them out but Jones's little army would protect them.

Suicide drills were stepped up. "Would you kill for me?" Jones often asked. In San Francisco the whole group was sometimes organized alphabetically to pledge their complete loyalty in death.

One day in Guyana, Jones filled a big vat with Kool-Aid and ordered all residents to take a cup and drink. The so-called "white night" had finally arrived. They were told to go out of the pavilion and lie down to die. A couple of women screamed and toppled over. Soon dozens went outside to die. It was a false alarm. There was no poison in the drink. Everyone suddenly realized it was only another drill, but the residents had to be prepared. Jones's enemies were "closing in."

"People's Temple is no stranger to persecution," one of their flyers said. "As a progressive group and outspoken against social and racial injustice, we have always known what it is to live in the shadow of threats, violence, and death. Our children have been harassed in their schools. Our pets have been tortured and left mutilated on our doorsteps."

In an atmosphere of hate whipped up by the press, a man called the temple numerous times saying he would shoot everyone who stepped out of the building. "We had to call for police protection," the publication stated.

In 1978, one of Jones's nurses, Joyce Parks, escorted two Jonestown residents to Caracas, Venezuela, for surgery. Once in Caracas, Joyce fled, leaving her husband and baby behind. Joyce was too fearful to tell her own husband of the planned escape. Bugs and eavesdropping devices were thought to be everywhere. "Dale is strong. I thought he would figure a way to get out. We were frightened," she explained. "Jim had us believing there was a CIA agent behind every banana tree."

The residents of Jonestown were now cut off from the outside world. All forms of communication were controlled. Commanards were told that Los Angeles had been abandoned because of severe drought. They were led to believe the Ku Klux Klan was marching in the open throughout San Francisco streets and that race wars had broken out across the country. Communards were told to work, work, work. The few tales that got out of Jonestown made it sound like Cambodia.

In 1978 relatives of the Jonestown members petitioned Cyrus Vance, U.S. Secretary of State and Forbes Burnham, the Prime Minister of Guyana. There was no success.

That fall I received a letter from Al Mills at the Human Freedom Center in Berkeley, California. He said that a "high-ranking government official" would be leading a group of people to Guyana.

They planned to take a medical doctor and a psychologist. The anonymous official was "in a position to demand entrance and insist on seeing certain selected members of the group."

Vicki and I watched anxiously and prayed for the expedition. It finally hit the papers. The anonymous official was Democratic Congressman Leo Ryan.

Five days after the group's departure from San Francisco International Airport the Jones affair exploded in all its ugliness. Everything that had been hidden and rumored surfaced into reality. Caught in the trap were the innocent members of the expedition. Newspaper headlines shouted that Ryan and his entourage had been ambushed by

191

residents of the "peaceful" Jonestown commune, and that at least five people were dead, including Ryan himself.

While I sat at my desk in Portland, Oregon, begging for someone to believe me, the Guyanese government moved troops into the Port Kaituma area. The dead Americans in Ryan's group were identified as NBC cameraman Robert Brown, NBC television reporter Don Harris, and *San Francisco Examiner* photographer Gregory Parks. Representative Leo J. Ryan, Democrat from California, was identified as the fifth ambush victim.

The targets had been eleven members of Ryan's original group and some sixteen Jonestown defectors who requested safe passage back to the United States. Mark Lane and Charles Garry, attorneys for People's Temple, accompanied Ryan to the Jonestown settlement but stayed behind when the group departed for Port Kaituma where a Guyana Airways charter flight was waiting to take them back to civilization. About a dozen gunmen took part in the massacre while Guyanese soldiers at the airport reportedly looked on without attempting to stop the killers.

Upon receiving word that Ryan had been killed, but that most of the defectors had escaped execution, Jones called his people together to participate in a mass suicide-communion which they had practiced many times before as a test of their loyalty to "Dad Jones." There was electricity in the air. All rehearsals were over.

And so, when Jones sounded his final shrieking alert over the settlement's much-used loudspeaker, it is likely that a large percentage of the town's residents were indeed ready and willing to die for their "father." Many, perhaps most by now, had no personality, no life, apart from People's Temple. "I like to have sex for several hours with an individual," Jones once bragged to my old girl friend. "In the process their personalities are destroyed and they become just barnyard animals."

"Everyone has to die," Jones told his followers from his throne-like chair in the main meeting hall. "If you love me as much as I love you, we must all die or be destroyed from the outside." He ordered that the babies and children be given the poison first.

A tape recording of the moment is filled with screaming babies and the shouts of Jones: "Mothers, control your children! Control your children! Put it way deep down the throat! Put it deep!" Jones evidently feared the babies might vomit the poison and live. Some babies were grabbed from their mothers and presented to camp nurses who used hypodermic needles to shoot streams of poison into the infants' mouths.

Some Jonestown disciples walked willingly to the stainless steel vat of poison. They drank a mixture of Kool-Aid and cyanide, concocted by camp doctor Lawrence Schanct. Some resisted, but were forced to drink. The ritual communion-suicide which they had practiced countless times was being carried out with insane determination.

It was taking too long, Jones decided. He stepped down from the platform which held his throne and swept through the crowd shouting, "Hurry, hurry, hurry!" A few frightened disciples managed to slip past the guards and into the jungle. Many children were already dead, and now the five-minute death potion was gripping the adults.

"Don't tell the children they are dying," Jones intoned. "Don't tell them it's painful. To die in revolutionary suicide is to live forever! We must die with dignity! We must all die!"

At least one devout cultist thought he could see the real reason behind the suicides. "We'll all die tonight," he said calmly, "but father will raise us from the dead tomorrow."

Three who escaped, a Jonestown resident named Odell Rhodes and attorneys Lane and Garry, said that Jones harangued his followers with a final sermon about "the dignity of death" and said they would all meet soon in "another place." The bizarre diatribe ended when Jones, chanting "Mother, mother, mother," put a pistol to his head and fired.

Survivors of the Port Kaituma airstrip slaughter, eight of whom were wounded, remained huddled near the edge of the runway, awaiting what they felt was the certain return of the murderers who earlier attacked them with automatic rifles and shotguns. The wounded were finally moved to a small army tent at the end of the runway. Four armed soldiers, who failed to intervene during the carnage, "guarded" the wounded victims. The rest of the group took shelter at a nearby bar, the Rum House, and recalled the events leading up to that day's tragedy.

Ryan's group initially had been denied entry into Jonestown, but the previous Friday Jones had relented, and now he welcomed the visitors as enthusiastically as he had previously shunned them.

Reporters were escorted around the community and were impressed by the cleanliness of the town and the apparent contentment of its multiracial populace. That evening they were entertained by a highly-talented band and deluged with comments about how happy folks were to be living in Jonestown.

It is hard to say why commune members presented such an Eden-like picture when Ryan and his investigative team first arrived at the settlement. Some may have been too frightened to say anything, but a more sobering explanation is that the cultists, by and large, no longer saw anything amiss in the character of Jonestown or their demonic leader. Whatever "Dad" Jones said was true, and whatever he said had to be done. It just had to be done.

A trip to a bar in Port Kaituma that evening introduced the group to a different outlook, however. Local Guyanese said there were guns, plenty of them, in "pacifist" Jonestown, and that the mysterious cult leader maintained a shotgun-wielding security team which he dubbed "the learning crew." Jonestown citizens who tried to leave were beaten and confined to a small storage box for days at a time. Newsman Don Harris also revealed that evening that a young man at the colony had handed him a slate containing four signatures and the desperate plea: "Please help me get out of Jonestown."

The following day, as the group prepared to leave Jonestown, others came forward to say they wanted to get out. Evidently fearful of retribution, they waited till the last minute to approach Ryan and the others.

*Washington Post* correspondent Charles Krause, who survived the airport bloodbath, said that in interviews held Friday and Saturday Jones became incoherent at times, and responded to accusations with increasing rage, despondency, and desperation. He hated violence, hated power, hated money, he insisted. "They" were pressing in from every side with lies and assassination plans. There was a conspiracy against him and People's Temple. "I might as well die," he said. "I wish somebody had shot me dead. Now we're substituting media smear for assassination." As more people were gathering to leave, Jones said they could go ahead and leave; the fewer people, the less responsibility he would have. "But they will try to destroy us. They always lie when they leave."

Jones took large amounts of pills, and claimed that all sorts of diseases were killing him, including cancer. (A San Francisco physician, Dr. Carlton Goodlet, later confirmed that Jones was seriously ill and was to enter a hospital for tests following Ryan's visit to the commune. He said no diagnosis had been made prior to the cult leader's death, however.)

Tensions increased, and there were at least two incidents of family members trying to forcibly dissuade relatives from leaving. Jonestown loyalists tried to put a good face on the situation, hugging defectors as they boarded a truck bound for Port Kaituma. Jones reportedly offered $5,000 for travel expenses.

Suddenly, members of the group heard shouting coming from the settlement's main meeting place. Don Sly, Neva's husband and the man she feared so much, took a knife and lunged at Congressman Ryan. Attorneys Charles Garry and Mark Lane intervened, and the attacker was cut during the scuffle. Ryan hurried to the truck, his shirt front splattered with blood. As quickly as possible, the refugees boarded the truck and rolled out of the compound.

Once at the airport, Ryan and his assistant, Jackie Speier, hurriedly checked people onto the two waiting planes. Ryan searched the people as they boarded, for there were rumors that one of the "defectors" might be a plant. Larry Leyton, who had exhibited somewhat suspicious behavior since the group's departure, was searched twice.

Dale Parks, the husband of the nurse who had escaped through Caracas several months before, was worried. He warned the congressman.

Parks was right. Jones had allegedly convinced Leyton to join the party, wait till the plane was in the air, then murder the pilot and assure the complete destruction of all on board. Meanwhile, at the Jonestown camp, Jones prophesied to his people: he had had a vision, Ryan's plane would crash.

There was a problem at Port Kaituma—there were too many defectors. Leyton would have to fall back on a second contingency.

Some of the group noticed that a People's Temple tractor and trailer rig was advancing toward the airplanes. They sensed trouble as the men on the tractor gestured ominously for a group of Guyanese bystanders to step aside.

Then came the first shot, followed quickly by dozens more. Those not already in the planes dove for cover under the aircraft or in the dense jungle growth beside the runway. The death squad passed through to finish off the wounded. They appeared to have no pattern for their executions, but would shoot some and simply leave others for dead.

Inside one of the planes, Patricia Parks, Dale's sister-in-law, lay dead. Dale wrestled with Larry Leyton for possession of a .38 revolver. Two others in the plane were wounded. Parks wrenched the gun away from Leyton and tried to shoot him with it, but the pistol failed to fire. Parks and Leyton were separated during the confusion surrounding the ambush, but Leyton returned to the plane when the shooting ended. Guyanese authorities took him into custody and charged him with murder.

Finally, about thirteen hours later, 100 Guyanese troops arrived from Georgetown, 150 miles away. The survivors were airlifted to Georgetown, and then on to Andrews Air Force Base near Washington.

In the days that followed, it seemed that all America's attention focused on the remote jungle "Eden" of Jim Jones. Evening news broadcasts devoted half the air time to coverage of the tragedy, and night after night a shocked nation watched and listened in near disbelief. The truth about Jonestown, as it turned out, was even worse than early rumors had indicated.

Initial estimates of the mass suicide toll proved to be inadequate. Soon the body count climbed to over 400. Meanwhile, reports of a 200-member hit squad, programmed to kill People's Temple defectors and high-ranking politicians, were emanating from the Human Freedom Center in Berkeley. Attorney Mark Lane, who escaped the Jonestown carnage with Charles Garry, contended that People's Temple was in the second phase of a four-phase assassination plot.

Stage one was the Jonestown suicide pact. Stage

two was the disavowal of wrongdoing by surviving cult leadership, with condemnation of the Jonestown debacle and, if necessary, of Jones himself. Stage three was to be the murder of disenfranchised members of People's Temple. The final stage would be the execution of public officials. Lane said a formerly high-ranking cult leader had given him this information just before Ryan's fact-finding group left for Guyana.

Grace Stoen who, with her husband Tim, had been trying to get their six-year-old son out of Jonestown for several months, said that the "mastermind" behind the assassination squad was a thirty-year-old woman masochist who inhabited a six-foot by four-foot closet in the People's Temple headquarters in San Francisco. Files which had been kept on temple defectors have disappeared, according to Stoen, along with the woman whom she described as a "frail, five-foot-seven loner." Loyal temple members in San Francisco vehemently denied that any such death squads existed. Members described themselves as "practical Christians."

In Guyana, the grim task of removing and identifying hundreds of suicide victims continued. Among the first bodies identified were Jones and another alleged mistress, Marie Katsaris. Rumors that the maniacal leader had substituted a stand-in double and fled in a special getaway boat were laid to rest when authorities positively identified the corpse's fingerprints as those of Rev. James Warren Jones.

Also found at the death site were about 800 U.S. passports belonging to Jonestown cultists, approximately forty automatic weapons and thousands of rounds of ammunition, plus gold, jewelry, and currency valued at around one million dollars. Several thousand dollars worth of uncashed Social Security checks, "donated" to Jonestown by senior citizens of the settlement, were also located.

Still, there was the nagging question: if the Jonestown population was really 1,200 as Jones claimed, where were the remaining survivors? After several days, only a few had emerged from jungle hiding places. Authorities speculated that some had been taken in by friendly Indian tribes in the area, others, perhaps, had been lost in the jungle.

Then came the unexpected and nightmarish solution. As U.S. and Guyanese troops labored to clear Jonestown of the bloated, decaying bodies, they discovered under the top layer of corpses yet another group of victims. These, explained a U.S. government spokesman, were the shells of the young children who had received the poison first and, consequently, were the first to die. Adult bodies on top had concealed the smaller corpses from searchers. The body count, they said, could go as high as seven or eight hundred.

One week following the Jonestown death orgy, U.S. Army burial teams loaded the last of the corpses on a helicopter.

The final count: 912 dead.

The exhausted men broke into applause and slapped one another on the back. Their job was over.

Among the dead was the baby of Dale and Joyce Parks. Lying next to Jones was a child which some said was the son of Tim and Grace Stoen. Jones had claimed the boy was his and in the end he had him.

At Dover Air Force Base, Delaware, the excruciating task of identifying cultists' unrecognizable remains continued as shipment after shipment of aluminum caskets arrived. The cost of the recovery operation was expected to reach nine million dollars.

In Georgetown, Guyana, an estimated eighty-four cult members (thirty-nine who fled into the jungle during the mass suicide, forty-five who were in Georgetown at the time of the tragedy) waited to be airlifted to Charleston Air Force Base in South Carolina. Five others were being held in connection with the Port Kaituma massacre and related killings.

Larry Leyton, the alleged "plant" who may have been ordered to bring down the plane carrying Ryan and the Jonestown defectors after it was airborne, was arrested at Port Kaituma immediately following the ambush.

Michael Prokes, a former Modesto, California, television reporter who had acted in a public relations capacity for Jones, and Tim Carter, from

Garden City, Idaho, were arrested by Guyana police in the jungle. They reportedly were carrying about $100,000 in cash and were armed. Carter's brother, Michael, was also apprehended.

A fifth man, Charles Beikman of Indianapolis, Indiana, was arrested on suspicion of killing a sect member and her three children in Georgetown after the mass suicide in Jonestown had ended.

Prokes and the two Carter brothers were later released. However, American officials said that criminal charges might possibly be filed against some of the ninety or so surviving cult members. They did not specify what charges might be filed, or against whom.

Prokes and the Carters revealed yet another bizarre twist to the complex Jonestown grotesquerie. Jones's alleged mistress, Marie Katsaris, gave them a heavy suitcase and two handguns and told them to deliver the case to "the embassy." The trio fled the scene of the suicide ritual, assuming that the suitcase was to be handed over to the American embassy in Georgetown. When they opened the case, however, they found approximately $500,000 and a note to the Soviet embassy. They stuffed about $100,000 in their pockets and buried the remainder. Prokes said they wrestled their way through the jungle and turned themselves in to police at Port Kaituma. They later returned with authorities to Jonestown where they helped identify bodies and directed police to the buried money.

Then came the discovery of a Jonestown document which revealed that the paranoid god of Jonestown was making plans to move his cult followers to Cuba, Russia, or some other place where he would be safe from imagined oppressors and assassins. Leaders of the commune had met with an official of the Soviet consulate at least twice, and the official allegedly indicated that a mass exodus from Guyana to the USSR could be arranged for Jonestown residents. The cash-filled suitcase evidently was part of a contingency plan to hasten the exodus once final approval came from Soviet authorities.

In the months that followed the meetings, Jones instituted mandatory study of the Russian language in the settlement, and his sermons made frequent reference to the possibility of moving the colony to a Communist country.

Jones, whose mental and physical health began deteriorating rapidly in the final year before the mass suicide, moved from a moderate socialist philosophy to radical Marxism. Already acutely fearful of threats, mostly imagined, against his person and his movement, Jones may have ordered the mass suicide after realizing that Ryan's death meant the end of his "revolutionary" vision to flee to Russia—"the promised land" (as Jones called it). It could also have meant the end of any revolutionary schemes.

A sealed note found on the cult commander's body, apparently written by a follower just prior to the ritual suicide, gave additional credence to this theory. "Dad," the note said, "I see no way out—I agree with your decision—I fear only that without you the world may not make it to communism. For my part I am more than tired of this wretched, merciless planet and the hell it holds for so many masses of beautiful people—thank you for the ONLY life I've known."

Held in Georgetown under house arrest, Prokes and the Carters were unwelcome among the other Jonestown refugees in the same hotel. Because Prokes had served as the cult's public information officer and was frequently involved in private conferences with Jones, survivors speculated that the three were members of a death squad organized to kill disloyal followers who refused to commit suicide.

The trio professed to be every bit as scared as the others, and Prokes insisted that although he was the cult's media representative he was not privy to inside information. Jones mistrusted him, he said, and although he was free to move in and out of Jonestown as he pleased, the cult leader may have suspected the former television reporter of being an outside agent.

Prokes said he knew nothing about rumors of "mass suicide practice" except that he knew they had taken place when he was not present. He also disclaimed knowledge of weapons arsenals and a storeroom containing potassium cyanide and other drugs which had been uncovered by Guyanese searchers. He praised the original ideals of the cult, which he said espoused social justice more than religion. When confronted with survivors' stories about macabre forms of punishment used in Jonestown, Prokes said he never saw any of those things going on. As for his own future, he said he would never follow another leader, but felt a need to "help people."

Jonestown escapees claimed Prokes was Jones's right-hand man, and "heir apparent" to the cult chieftain's throne.

Tim and Mike Carter said simply that they were "scared as hell," and wanted to go home.

It seemed that news from the Guyana tragedy was finally petering out. Then came the sudden, shocking deaths of San Francisco Mayor George Moscone, who had in 1976 appointed Jones to the city's housing authority and was perhaps closer to him than any other political figure had been, and Supervisor Harvey Milk, a declared homosexual who carried the political banner for the city's gay community.

It was initially feared that the pre-programmed People's Temple death "angels" had begun their carnage. Thirty-five minutes after the shooting deaths of Moscone and Milk, however, a former supervisor named Dan White turned himself in to authorities and confessed to the killings. There was no reason to link White to the death squad stories, police said, for White had never had any connection with People's Temple.

But some temple-watchers refused to believe it. "They'll find a connection there somewhere," said one. "It's too much of a coincidence."

# epilogue

## *Mysteries That Remain*

In the aftermath of Jonestown several mysteries remained. A few of these have been cleared up. People's Temple attorney Charles Garry told me that Private Detective Mazzore had indeed been employed by the temple. Our fears in this bizarre story had too often proved to be true.

One mystery yet unsolved is the Soviet-Cuban connection. What was Jones's long-range plan for Guyana? Was Jones planning to fulfill his boast to become a national leader, a head of state? Some temple members believe so. Was Jones planning to use his commune as a base for Cuban-sponsored guerilla warfare in nearby Venezuela? Or perhaps he was planning to carve his own statehood from land disputed by Venezuela and Guyana? Were the

Soviet and Cuban governments exploiting Jones's egomania by encouraging him, hoping to provide an incident which would be embarrassing to the United States?

As far-fetched as this all sounds, consider the following facts which are in the public domain. Even the Chinese are involved.

1. Like Hitler, Jones had announced his intentions long before he carried them out. Jones took his prophecies and ideas very seriously and ruthlessly made sure they were fulfilled. Like Hitler, people tended to make excuses for Jones and rationalized his more outrageous claims.

2. Jones thought of himself as a future world leader and encouraged his entourage to propagate that view. We were told that one day Jones would talk with presidents and kings as an equal.

3. For years the Cubans have been trying to export their revolution to South America.

4. Jones was a Marxist who had numerous contacts with officials of both the Soviet and Cuban governments. Cult members were told that if the need should arise, arrangements had been made to evacuate them all to Cuba or the Soviet Union. In the last few months of Jonestown, children were being taught the Russian language.

5. Jonestown was founded in an area which was disputed by both the Guyanese and Venezuelan governments.

6. The People's Republic of China had agreed to

build a hydraulic plant near Jonestown. This project had been hotly protested by Venezuela who finally agreed to it, provided that the power generated would be shared with them as well as Guyana.

7. Crates of arms were shipped from San Francisco to Jonestown. Large amounts of foreign currencies and gold were kept on the compound.

8. Jones often took commendations from American political leaders and turned them into apparent endorsements in the eyes of foreign leaders. It gave him credibility with the Guyanese. It may have impressed the Soviets.

9. A Russian-speaking emissary had visited Jones just weeks before the suicide.

10. The Soviets reacted to the suicides immediately. While our own state department was confused and stunned, the Soviets responded quickly and clearly, divorcing themselves entirely from the American Marxist. Russians used it as an example of American insanity.

11. Two temple members were sent out by Jones prior to the mass suicide. They were to deliver a suitcase to the Soviet embassy in Georgetown. Inside was $500,000, some documents, and weapons.

CONCLUSIONS: Very combustible elements were present—the Chinese, the Russians, the Cubans, the Venezuelans and the Guyanese. Was Jones, in his egomania, planning to work one force against the other and come away with something of his own? Did the Soviets lead him to believe they would provide military assistance, recognition, and an umbrella if he should declare statehood?

Another mystery involves money. Jones often warned associates that governments and courts can freeze bank accounts. One large source of cash was found in Jonestown. It included millions of dollars. Are there others? Two of Jones's men were found leaving Jonestown with half a million dollars. Did anyone get out who has not been found?

A former business manager of People's Temple has warned that cash is probably available. An investigation is being conducted into the removal of eight million dollars from Swiss bank accounts.

Consider the cave where money and supplies were kept in case of nuclear war. Bonnie Thielmann says the cave was cleaned out but other sources say it was only moved.

Then there is the mystery of murder. Were any of the mysterious deaths within the family legend actually murder? As this book goes to press a grand jury hearing is taking place. Based upon my information to the FBI, Faith Kice and Linda Sweeney, former Jones mistresses, have been taken into protective custody and are telling all. Indictments for murder may be forthcoming. But what can be proved? Were the deaths coincidental? If the events in Guyana finally cause inquiry into these deaths are there persons living who can be implicated?

Will there be further murders as Neva Sly and others warned? Is there a post-suicide hit squad? Are assassinations of San Francisco Mayor Moscone and City Commissioner Harvey Milk related to the Jones incident? What was the relationship between San Francisco District Attorney Joe Freitas and Jim Jones?

Another mystery surrounds the death of Jones. Was he planning a getaway? Was he murdered by another temple member who, seeing the horror of the suicides, decided that Jones should not survive? Perhaps Jones had sent the money supply to the Russian embassy to arrange for his own departure.

Finally there is the most baffling mystery of all: Why did it happen?

Since Guyana's tragedy there have been angry demands that American authorities do something immediately to stop the growth of cults. The Justice Department and Federal Bureau of Investigation have received many such requests from members of congress as well as concerned private individuals, but both departments said any such investigations would violate freedom of religion guarantees in the constitution.

While legal minds began trying to ascertain the consequences of cult investigations, America was confronted head-on with figures that said up to 10 percent of Americans may be involved in fringe cults whose doctrines involve everything from Satan worship to UFO idolatry. Up to 5,000 new cults may have been organized in the last decade, and scholars estimate the number of adherents at between twenty and twenty-six million.

Our American Constitution has never been tested as it has in recent years. The concept of a free press is colliding with the promise of a fair trial and now the pendulum may be swinging away from freedom of religion. I hope not. It was through Christ that I became free from the hold of People's Temple.

Psychologists and theologians are answering theories about why people get drawn into cults, and are also making some statistical observations.

The most susceptible age group for cults at the present time is the 18-24 range. The groups usually appeal to individuals with a need for absolute answers and externally imposed disciplines. They normally rely on intensive indoctrination in secluded settings to retain new recruits. Almost all are characterized by a fanatical commitment among its followers, and the requirement of absolute loyalty to a specific, powerful leader.

Some blamed a mechanistic, unconcerned society. Others cited the breakdown of the family and lack of moral and ethical guidelines within the society. At least one expert said the main villain was the jungle, which isolated Jones's followers from the rest of the world and made them lose a proper perspective of their actions and life style.

But perhaps the most practical advice came from

the Vatican newspaper, *L'Osservatore Romano*, which referred to a warning that was voiced nearly 2,000 years ago:

> For false Christs and false prophets shall rise, and shall shew signs and wonders, to seduce, if it were possible, even the elect. But take ye heed: behold, I have foretold you all things. (Mark 13:22, 23)

> Wherefore if they shall say unto you, Behold, he is in the desert; go not forth: behold, he is in the secret chambers; believe it not. (Matt. 24:26)

# APPENDIX A

# PEOPLE'S TEMPLE—PEOPLE'S TOMB

PETITION ENTREATING SECRETARY OF STATE CYRUS
VANCE TO PROTECT THE HUMAN RIGHTS OF UNITED
STATES CITIZENS IN "JONESTOWN", GUYANA

TO: HONORABLE CYRUS VANCE, SECRETARY OF STATE OF THE UNITED
    STATES OF AMERICA

From: "Concerned Relatives": Parents and relatives of child-
      ren and adults under the control of Rev. James Warren
      Jones at "Jonestown", Northwest District, Guyana, South
      America

Date: May 10, 1978

We, the undersigned 57 petitioners, are the grief-stricken
parents and relatives of the hereinafter-designated U. S. citizens now residing in the Cooperative Republic of Guyana, South
America. We respectfully entreat you to attend to the following
facts:

1. More than 1,000 United States citizens, including our
relatives, are now living in Guyana, South America at a jungle
encampment named "Jonestown", whose leader is Jim Jones, also a
citizen of the United States.

2. We have evidence that Jonestown has turned into a "concentration camp" in which the rights of its residents under the
U. S. Constitution, the United Nations Charter, the Guyana Constitution, and the Guyana Penal Code are being seriously and systematically violated by Jim Jones. The facts supporting this

sad conclusion include the following:

 a. The stationing of guards around Jonestown to prevent anyone leaving the encampment without Jones' permission;

 b. The confiscation by Jones of all passports and monies to prevent anyone from buying an airline ticket home and from being cleared at Tímehri International Airport to leave Guyana;

 c. The requirement that no resident of Jonestown be permitted to leave the encampment except on business for Jones, and then only in the company of others required to spy and report back to Jones;

 d. The prohibition of long distance telephone calls to the United States and all other forms of free communication;

 e. The censoring of all incoming and outgoing mail;

 f. The prohibition of anyone leaving Jones' organization, Peoples Temple, under threat of death.

 These are _facts_, and they are documented by eye-witness accounts in the notarized affidavits of Yulanda Crawford and Steven A. Katsaris attached hereto. (In addition, we have recently been advised and believe, but need an investigation to verify, that Jones has installed barbed-wire fences and has also installed a closed-circuit television system for internal surveillance.)

 4. On April 12, 1978 we served on Peoples Temple officials in San Francisco a document which cited, by Article and Section number, the particular provisions of the Universal Declaration of Human Rights (guaranteed by Article 55 of the United Nations Charter) and of the Guyana Constitution being violated. This

# PEOPLE'S TEMPLE—PEOPLE'S TOMB

document is entitled, "Accusation of Human Rights Violations by Rev. James Warren Jones Against Our Children and Relatives at the Peoples Temple Jungle Encampment in Guyana, South America."

5.  On April 19, 1978 we sent a copy of the aforesaid Accusation to each of the following officials of the Department of State:

  a. Hon. Cyrus Vance, Secretary of State;

  b. Hon. Warren Christopher, Deputy Secretary of State;

  c. Hon. Douglas Bennet, Assistant Secretary of State for Congressional Relations;

  d. Hon. Patricia Derian, Assistant Secretary of State for Human Rights;

  e. Hon. Hodding Carter III, Assistant Secretary of State for Public Affairs; and

  f. Hon. Stephen Dobrenchuk, Chief of Emergency and Protection Services Division for Department of State.

6.  We are herewith submitting today a document entitled, "PETITION ENTREATING PRIME MINISTER FORBES BURNHAM TO STOP REV. JAMES WARREN JONES FROM FURTHER VIOLATIONS OF THE HUMAN RIGHTS OF OUR RELATIVES IN GUYANA." We ask that you read it carefully, particularly the quotations from Peoples Temple on a "decision" to die, and a "unanimous vote" to put "our lives on the line." We ask that you then transmit the same through official State Department channels to the Honorable Forbes Burnham.

NOW, THEREFORE, WE RESPECTFULLY ask that you, HONORABLE CYRUS VANCE, in your capacity as SECRETARY OF STATE FOR THE UNITED STATES, take the following action to protect the human and legal rights of the United States citizens in Jonestown, Guyana, before it is too late:

1. Immediately transmit to the Honorable Forbes Burnham, Prime Minister of Guyana, the enclosed petition dated May 10, 1978 addressed to him.

2. Immediately order the Honorable John R. Burke, United States Ambassador to Guyana, to launch a continuing investigation of Jonestown, including the placement of U. S. Embassy personnel in Jonestown to protect the legal rights of the U. S. citizens there.

3. Officially request on behalf of the United States Government that Prime Minister Burnham take the action requested in our aforesaid petition addressed to him.

4. Officially request all international agencies concerned with human rights to investigate and monitor the activities of Jim Jones which violate such rights, including the United Nations, the International Commission of Human Rights, the International Red Cross, Amnesty International, the International Commission of Jurists.

5. Notify our spokesman, Steven A. Katsaris, Trinity School, 915 West Church Street, Ukiah, California 95482 (telephone 707-462-8721) of your willingness to take the action herein requested.

RESPECTFULLY SUBMITTED,

CONCERNED RELATIVES

(Summarized Listing of Petitioners Attached to Enclosed Petition to Guyana Prime Minister Forbes Burnham)

**PEOPLES
TEMPLE**
OF THE
DISCIPLES OF CHRIST
*Jim Jones,
Pastor*

March 14, 1978

*"For I was an hungred
and ye gave me meat;
I was thirsty
and ye gave me drink;
I was a stranger
and ye took me in;
Naked, and ye clothed me;
I was sick and ye visited me;
I was in prison,
and ye came unto me.*

*"Then shall the righteous
Answer him, saying,*

*When saw we thee an hungred
And fed thee?
Or thirsty
And gave thee drink?
When saw we thee a stranger
And took thee in?
Or naked, and clothed thee
Or when saw we thee sick?
Or in prison,
And came unto thee?*

*"Verily I say unto you,
Inasmuch as ye have done it
Unto one of the least of these...
Ye have done it unto me"*

Matthew 25:35-40

TO ALL U.S. SENATORS AND MEMBERS OF CONGRESS:

We at Peoples Temple have been the subject of harassment by several agencies of the U.S. Government, and are rapidly reaching the point at which patience is exhausted. Radical Trotskyite elements which defected from our organization when we refused to follow their violent course have been orchestrating a campaign against us. Two of these, Michael Cartmell and Jim Cobb, were actually discovered making ammunition several years ago. These same two persons have boasted about knowing persons in the IRS and FCC and using them to get back at Peoples Temple. They also vowed recently to several witnesses that they would see to it that our group of over 1,000 U.S. citizens (currently conducting a highly successful agricultural project in Guyana) were starved out by having funds cut off from the U.S. To date, several agencies have been attempting various forms of harrassment. First was the Social Security, which tried to deny legitimate beneficiaries of their rights by cutting off all checks that were coming to Guyana. Through the intervention of various government officials, we were able to have this reinstated as it should have been.

Now, however, we see that the IRS and Treasury Dept. and even the Federal Communications Commission, are trying to initiate ways to cut off our lifelines. The FCC has suddenly decided to pursue a very minor complaint that was registered a year ago. It is clear that the intention is to disrupt our essential medium of communication, amateur radio. Each week we contact thousands of amateur radio operators; contacts and consultation with doctors in the U.S. have literally saved lives and have engendered tremendous goodwill in this part of the world. We consistently praise the U.S. over the airways and remain entirely supportive of U.S. policy in the Caribbean and around the world, especially with non-aligned nations. It seems utterly cruel to deprive such a large group of Americans of their only means of quick communication with the U.S. We cannot believe that you would want to see this, nor would you in any way condone such an organized effort to "starve out" hundreds of U.S. citizens, who are seeking to live in peace and be a credit to the U.S. elsewhere. These same agencies and elements in the press would seek to destroy any progressive thinking official.

Our cooperative project in Guyana has been cited by people the world over as an example of a new image for the U.S. This project and the efforts of Peoples Temple were recently praised in the magazine One World, a publication of the World Council of Churches. Even Russia's New Times magazine has praised this work and done so in spite of our strong support of Russian people of Jewish descent, an obvious disagreement. We receive letters weekly from Russia, as well as from people in other parts of the world who have heard of the project, offering advice and assistance. In fact, several overtures have been made from Russia, which sees our current harassment as a form of political persecution. We do not want to take assistance from any people nor do we want to become an international issue. We also do not intend to be starved out by having our legitimately earned income cut off through the efforts of Trotskyite people and embittered malcontents. We have no political aspirations whatsoever. Jim Jones has spent the last 8 months working to develop the project in Guyana. We wish to continue to do so unmolested and unhampered. This project has done a great deal of practical good for the U.S., not only in promoting a positive image in a place where many of the populace have more of a left leaning, but also in a very tangible way financially. The amount of tax dollars we have saved the U.S. by taking people off welfare and off SSI and steering some from inevitable lives of crime would total conservatively in the hundreds of thousands. More importantly than that, lives have been saved that would have been meant for destruction. It seems cruel that anyone would want to escalate this type of bureaucratic harrassment into an international issue, but it is equally evident that people cannot forever be continually harrassed and be badgered by such tactics without seeking alternatives that have been presented. I can say without hesitation that we are devoted to a decision that it is better even to die than to be constantly harrassed from one continent to the next. I hope you can look into this matter and protect the right of over 1,000 people from the U.S. to live in peace.

223

Sincerely,
Jim Jones
Pastor

# PEOPLE'S TEMPLE—PEOPLE'S TOMB

AFFIDAVIT OF YOLANDA D. A. CRAWFORD SHOWING

THE TEACHINGS AND PRACTICES OF REV. JAMES

WARREN JONES IN GUYANA, SOUTH AMERICA

I, Yolanda D. A. Crawford, certify as follows:

1. I was in Guyana, South America as a member of Peoples Temple from April 1, 1977 until June 29, 1977. Rev. James Warren Jones ("Jim Jones"), the leader of Peoples Temple, was in Guyana most of April and during the latter part of June, at which times I witnessed the following statements and practices by him.

2. Jim Jones said that the United States is the "most evil" nation in the world, referring to its political and industrial leaders as "capitalistic pigs". He said he would rather have his people dead than live in the United States.

3. Jim Jones prior to June said that people would be coming to live in Guyana for a temporary period of time. In June Jim Jones stated that the people he brings over from the United States will be staying in Guyana "permanently".

4. Jim Jones said that nobody will be permitted to leave Jonestown and that he was going to keep guards stationed around Jonestown to keep anybody from leaving. He said that he had guns and that if anyone tries to leave they will be killed ("offed") and their bodies will be left in the jungle and "we can say that we don't know what happened to you." He also said, "I can get a hit man for fifty dollars. It's not hard for me to get a hit man anywhere."

EXHIBIT B

224

5. While still in the United States, Jim Jones asked the Temple members to turn all their guns over to him. I also saw ammunition being packed in crates for shipment to Guyana addressed to Peoples Temple from San Francisco. I heard Jim Jones say, "If anyone tries to start anything, we are ready and prepared to die for our cause."

6. Jim Jones said that black people and their sympathizers were going to be destroyed in the United States, that "the Ku Klux Klan is marching in the streets of San Francisco, Los Angeles, and cities back east". There was "fighting in the streets, and the drought in California is so bad, Los Angeles is being deserted".

7. Jim Jones said that everyone should turn in their passports and all their money to him, that nobody is to visit any local Guyanese people unless on a "mission" and in the company of other Temple members, that nobody is to make any telephone calls to relatives, that nobody was to send any mail to the United States without first getting it "cleared". All incoming mail was first received by Temple secretaries and read before being shown to the person addressed.

8. Jim Jones said that "I will lay my body down for this cause" and asked others to make the same promise, which they did by a show of hands, and also asked them to commit themselves to kill anyone attempting to hurt him.

9. Jim Jones ordered all of us to break our ties with families. He said that our highest and only loyalty should be "the cause", and that the only reason for staying in touch with our families was to collect inheritances when "they died off" and to keep them pacified "so as not to make trouble for the cause".

10. Jim Jones ordered us to "report" on one another to prevent "treason". His technique was to have everyone report to him (or his two or three most trusted leaders) all suspicious talk or behavior of others.

11. Jim Jones ordered people punished when they broke his rules. The punishments included food-deprivation, sleep-deprivation, hard labor, and eating South American hot peppers. I saw a teenager, Tommy Bogue, being forced to eat hot peppers at a public meeting.

12. So far as I know, only one person (Leon Brosheard) out of 850 or more residents has dared to leave Jonestown since my mother, husband and I left on June 29, 1977. Before Jim Jones allowed me to leave, I was forced to promise him I would never speak against the church, and that if I did I would lose his "protection" and be "stabbed in the back". Furthermore, Jim Jones ordered me to sign a number of self-incriminating papers, including a statement that I was against the government of Guyana, that I had plotted against that government, that I was part of the PPP (Peoples Progressive Party), which is the opposition party in Guyana, and that I had come to Guyana to help the PPP. Jim Jones said the reason for signing those papers was to discredit me if I ever decided to leave the movement "and talk". Also, before leaving for Guyana, I was ordered to fabricate a story and sign it stating that I killed someone and threw the body in the ocean. I was told that if I ever caused Jim Jones trouble, he would give that statement to the police. He further intimidated me and others in the congregation by saying, "I, (Jim Jones) have Mafia connections, and they will stand with me all the way."

-4-

13. I heard him state to the congregation in Guyana that Marshall Kilduff, who wrote the first articles exposing him, was dead. He said, "The angels have taken care of him". We all knew the "angels" were his people who would do you in if you crossed Jim Jones.

14. Jim Jones ordered all telephone calls to relatives in the United States to be made in the presence of Temple members and after coaching. When my mother tried to call her brother in the United States and get him to stop criticizing the Temple, Jim Jones stood by her side and told her everything she was to say and then faulted her for not being forceful enough. He ordered us to tell our relatives in the United States to stop criticizing him or we would not be allowed to return home.

15. On numerous occasions I was in the congregation when he told us "I am God" and "there is no other God, and religion is the opium of the people." He stated he used religion only to get to the masses.

16. I recall several instances of Jim Jones stating he could silence critics or defectors by accusing them of being homosexuals, child abusers, terrorists or sexual deviates.

I declare under penalty of perjury that the foregoing is true and correct. Executed at San Francisco, California on April 10, 1978.

_Yolanda R.A. Crawford_
YOLANDA D. A. CRAWFORD

# PEOPLE'S TEMPLE—PEOPLE'S TOMB

Guyana

PETITION ENTREATING PRIME MINISTER FORBES BURNHAM
TO STOP REV. JAMES WARREN JONES FROM FURTHER VIO-
LATIONS OF THE HUMAN RIGHTS OF OUR RELATIVES IN

GUYANA

TO: HONORABLE FORBES BURNHAM, PRIME MINISTER OF THE COOPERA-
TIVE REPUBLIC OF GUYANA, SOUTH AMERICA

From: "Concerned Relatives": Parents and relatives of children and adults under the control of Rev. James Warren
Jones at "Jonestown", Northwest District, Guyana

Date: May 10, 1978

We, the undersigned 57 petitioners, are the grief-stricken
parents and relatives of the hereinafter-designated persons now
living in your country. We respectfully entreat you to attend
to the following facts:

1. In June 1977 Rev. James Warren Jones ("Jim Jones")
left the United States for Guyana as he was about to be exposed
in the press for fraud, brutality to children, and taking prop-
erties by false pretenses. Jim Jones has never returned to the
United States to answer these charges.

2. Since June 1977 Jim Jones has induced more than 1,000
United States citizens to become permanent residents of Guyana
at his jungle encampment leased from your government. He calls
this encampment "Jonestown".

3. Jim Jones at this moment is flagrantly and systematic-

ally carrying out the following acts and abuses on all Jonestown residents, including our relatives:

a. Stations guards around Jonestown and threatens the residents with death if they attempt to leave;

b. Confiscates their passports and money;

c. Employs physical intimidation and psychological coercion as part of a mind-programming campaign aimed at destroying family ties, discrediting belief in God, and causing contempt for the United States of America, as well as for all other nation states, including Guyana;

d. Deprives them of their rights to privacy, free speech, freedom of association, and freedom of movement by:

    (1) Prohibiting telephone calls;

    (2) Prohibiting individual contacts with all "outsiders", including Guyanese;

    (3) Censoring all incoming and outgoing mail;

    (4) Extorting silence from relatives in the U.S. by threats to stop all communication;

    (5) Preventing our children from seeing us when we travel to Guyana (five of us have tried).

4. The foregoing acts are documented in the "Accusation of Human Rights Violations by Rev. James Warren Jones Against Our Children and Relatives at the Peoples Temple Jungle Encampment in Guyana, South America", a copy of which is attached. These acts of Jim Jones are a clear violation of the Guyanese Constitution and of the Universal Declaration of Human Rights, as quoted in the aforesaid Accusation. The physical intimidation is a violation of the penal code of Guyana.

5.  On April 11, 1978 we served the aforesaid Accusation
on Peoples Temple officials in San Francisco.  The Accusation
set forth a number of demands for relief, including a demand
that Jones permit and encourage our relatives to return to the
United States for a one-week visit home at our expense, return
fare being guaranteed.

6.  On April 12, 1978 we sent two copies of this Accusation
to you as Prime Minister of Guyana.  One copy was sent via the
Guyanese Embassy in Washington, D. C., and the other directly
to Georgetown, Guyana.  In our cover letter we asked you, as
"the one person in the world with power" over Jones, to take
action to stop his violations of human rights.  We have received
no response from you.

7.  On April 17, 1978 Jim Jones responded to our demands
for relief by staging a press conference in the office of his
attorney in San Francisco, wherein our relatives in Jonestown
read scripts over a radio-phone network praising "the integrity,
honesty, and bravery" of Jim Jones and falsely denouncing us as
child molesters, sexual deviates, dope addicts, and terrorists,
as well as manifesting other symptoms of mind-programming.  (In
order to show the falsity of these charges, Steven Katsaris on
May 2, 1978 voluntarily submitted himself to a professional polygraph examination.  The report, dated May 3 and attached hereto,
concludes:  "It is the opinion of the examiner, based on Katsaris' polygraph charts, that he is telling the truth.")

# PEOPLE'S TEMPLE—PEOPLE'S TOMB

8. On April 18, 1978 Jones intimated once again a threat so chilling as to be incomprehensible to the average decent person. In our Accusation we had demanded Jones clarify the following sentence in a March 14, 1978 letter on Peoples Temple stationery addressed "to all U. S. Senators and Members of Congress":

> "I can say without hesitation that we are
> devoted to a decision that it is better even
> to die than be constantly harrassed from one
> continent to the next."

On April 18 Jones issued a Press Release on Peoples Temple stationery with the following "clarification" (page 4):

> "And we, likewise, affirm that before we will
> submit quietly to the interminable plotting
> and persecution of this politically motivated
> conspiracy, we will resist actively, putting
> our lives on the line, if it comes to that.
> This has been the unanimous vote of the col-
> lective community here in Guyana."

9. On April 26, 1978 we served an advance version of this Petition on the Honorable Joseph D'Olivera, Honorary Consul for the Cooperative Republic of Guyana, Los Angeles, California.

10. We respectfully submit to you, Mr. Prime Minister, that the foregoing evidence shows that Jonestown, Guyana has taken on the characteristics of a "concentration camp", and that you, as the leader of Guyana, would do well to analyze the mentality of its leader so as to anticipate its potential for causing extreme damage to Guyana's reputation in the international community.

NOW, THEREFORE, WE RESPECTFULLY ask that you, HONORABLE FORBES BURNHAM, in your capacity as PRIME MINISTER OF GUYANA, take the following action to protect the human and legal rights of our relatives in Guyana before it is too late:

1.   Immediately order the Minister of Home Affairs and the Commissioner of Police to launch an ongoing investigation into Jones' violations of the Guyanese Penal Code and Constitution.

2.   Immediately order "Bishop Jim Jones" (as he presents himself to you) to cease and desist from the unlawful acts itemized in the attached Accusation, with particular orders for him to:

  a. Remove all guards stationed around Jonestown;

  b. Return to our relatives their passports and money;

  c. Permit them to mix with the local Guyanese as individuals;

  d. Permit them to make telephone calls to us in private at our expense when in Georgetown;

  e. Permit them to receive all mail individually addressed to them, and to read the same in private;

  f. Permit them to mail letters they write in private without being opened by Jones or his staff.

3.   Immediately order Jones to permit and encourage our relatives to return to the United States for a one-week home visit at our expense, so as to test whether or not they are being held against their will, upon our guarantee of return fare should they choose to return.

4.   Immediately order Jones to abide by the lawful orders of courts in the United States with respect to the custody of our relatives.

5.   If Jim Jones refuses to abide by your orders, expel him from Guyana so that Jonestown can become a democratic society in accordance with the Guyana Constitution.

6.  Notify our spokesman, Steven A. Katsaris, Trinity School, 915 West Church Street, Ukiah, California 95482 (telephone 707-462-8721) of your willingness to protect the human and legal rights of our relatives.

> RESPECTFULLY SUBMITTED,
>
> CONCERNED RELATIVES
>
> (Summarized Listing of Petitioners Attached)

# PEOPLE'S TEMPLE—PEOPLE'S TOMB

## HARMAN & SHAHEEN
### associates, Inc.

A PROFESSIONAL POLYGRAPH CORPORATION
Members: American Polygraph Association, California Association of Polygraph Examiners

GEORGE W. HARMAN
1182 MARKET STREET
SAN FRANCISCO 94102
415-863-5351

ROBERT S. SHAHEEN
586 N. FIRST STREET
SAN JOSE 95112
408-292-5423

CONFIDENTIAL REPORT:          May 3, 1978          No. P-9019

Mr. Timothy Oliver Stoen
Attorney At Law
120 Montgomery Street
San Francisco, California

On May 2, 1978, Steven A. Katsaris voluntarily came to this office for a polygraph examination. The main issue under consideration involved allegations of sexual molestation made against him by his daughter, Maria Katsaris. Maria is presently with the People's Temple Church in Guyana. During Mr. Katsaris' attempts to get his daughter away from this church, the allegations of sexual molestation were made by some of the officials of the People's Temple Church. No specific, public statements along this line were made by Maria Katsaris. Among other charges made against Katsaris by the People's Temple Church was the statement that he was involved with a right-wing congressman in a conspiracy to destroy People's Temple Church.

During Mr. Katsaris' pre-test interview, he maintained he has never made any sexual advances whatsoever toward his daughter, Maria. He also insisted that he has never been involved in any conspiracy with a congressman to destroy People's Temple Church.

There were no significant emotional disturbances indicative of deception reflected in Mr. Katsaris' polygraph charts when he answered "No" to the following test questions:

"Did you ever make any sexual advances toward Maria Katsaris?"

"Did you ever try to have sexual intercourse with your daughter, Maria?"

"Did you ever sexually fondle any part of Maria's body?"

"Did you ever plan with any congressman to destroy People's Temple Church?"

It is the opinion of the examiner, based on Katsaris' polygraph charts, that he is telling the truth on the above-listed questions.

Yours very truly,

HARMAN & SHAHEEN ASSOCIATES, INC.

George W. Harman

GH:rg

This report is furnished by this agency at the request of the client named above for his exclusive information only, and for no other reason or purpose. It is strictly confidential, and communication to other parties is the responsibility of the client.

234

# PEOPLE'S TEMPLE—PEOPLE'S TOMB

May 10, 1978

SUMMARY LISTING OF PETITIONERS WITH RELATIVES IN JONESTOWN, GUYANA

| Name of Relative at Jonestown | Age | Petitioners to Forbes Burnham and Cyrus Vance | Relationship to Petitioner |
|---|---|---|---|
| 1. Wagner, Mark | 16 | Richard Wagner (San Francisco) | Son |
| 2. Harris, Liane | 21 | Sherwin Harris (Lafayette) | Daughter |
| | | Elizabeth Harris (Lafayette) | Sister |
| 3. Ponts, Donna | 15 | Don Ponts (Ukiah) | Daughter |
| | | Cynthia Beam (Ventura) | Half-sister |
| 4. Oliver, William S. | 18 | Howard Oliver (San Francisco) | Son |
| | | Beverly Oliver (San Francisco) | Son |
| 5. Oliver, Bruce H. | 20 | Howard Oliver & Beverly Oliver | Son |
| 6. Katsaris, Maria | 24 | Steven A. Katsaris (Ukiah) | Daughter |
| 7. Rozynko, Michael | 20 | Sandy Rozynko Mills (Oakland) | Brother |
| | | Steve Mills (Oakland) | Bros.-in-law |
| 8. Rozynko, Chris | 22 | Steve Mills & Sandy Rozynko Mills | (Same) |
| 9. Rozynko, Joyce | 54 | Sandy Rozynko Mills | Mother |
| | | Steve Mills | Mother-in-law |
| 10. Stoen, John Victor | 6 | Grace Stoen (San Francisco) | Son |
| | | Timothy O. Stoen (San Francisco) | Son |
| 11. Sly, Mark A. | 17 | Neva Jean Sly (San Francisco) | Son |
| 12. Sly, Donald E. | 42 | Neva Jean Sly | Husband |
| 13. Houston, Patricia | 14 | Robert H. Houston (San Bruno) | Grandchild |
| | | Nadyne L. Houston (San Bruno) | Grandchild |
| | | Carol Boyd | Niece |
| 14. Houston, Judy Lynn | 13 | Robert & Nadyne Houston; Carol Boyd | (Same) |
| 15. Kerns, Carol Ann | 19 | Ruth Reinhardt (Davis) | Sister |
| | | Phil Kerns (Portland, Oregon) | Sister |
| | | Dolly Petersen (Riverside) | Grandchild |
| 16. Kerns, Ellen Louise | 51 | Ruth Reinhardt & Phil Kerns | Mother |
| | | Dolly Petersen | Daughter |
| 17. Harris, Magnolia | 61 | Sylvia White (San Francisco) | Mother |
| | | Leinaola White (San Francisco) | Grandmother |
| 18. Lopez, Vincent | 17 | Walter Jones (San Francisco) | Legal Guardian |
| 19. Simon, Marcia | 22 | Leon Simon (Oakland) | Daughter |
| 20. Simon, Barbara | 22 | Leon Simon | Daughter |
| 21. Johnson, Berda T. | 88 | Frances Baxter (Los Angeles) | Mother |

HUMAN RIGHTS ABUSES BY JIM JONES (CONTINUED)

| Name of Relative at Jonestown | Age | Petitioners to Forbes Burnham and Cyrus Vance | Relationship to Petitioner |
|---|---|---|---|
| 22. Griffith, Mary M. | 52 | Rose Davis (San Francisco)<br>Carnella Truss (San Francisco)<br>Louise Blanchard (San Francisco) | Aunt<br>Mother<br>Sister |
| 23. Cobb, John | 18 | James Cobb, Jr. (San Francisco) | Brother |
| 24. Cobb, Brenda | 15 | James Cobb, Jr. | Sister |
| 25. Cobb, Sandra | 21 | James Cobb, Jr. | Sister |
| 26. Cobb, Joel | 12 | James Cobb, Jr. | Brother |
| 27. Cobb, Christine | | James Cobb, Jr. | Mother |
| 28. Brown, Ava | 26 | James Cobb, Jr. | Sister |
| 29. Brown, John (Jones) | 28 | James Cobb, Jr. | Brother-in-law |
| 30. Touchette, Charles | 47 | Mickey Touchette (San Francisco)<br>Marvin Swinney (South Carolina) | Father<br>Brother-in-law |
| 31. Touchette, Joyce | 45 | Mickey Touchette<br>Marvin Swinney | Mother<br>Sister |
| 32. Touchette, Al | 23 | Mickey Touchette<br>Marvin Swinney | Brother<br>Nephew |
| 33. Touchette, Michael | 25 | Mickey Touchette<br>Marvin Swinney | Brother<br>Nephew |
| 34. Touchette, Michelle | 19 | Mickey Touchette<br>Marvin Swinney | Sister<br>Niece |
| 35. Swinney, Cleve | 65 | Mickey Touchette<br>Marvin Swinney | Grandfather<br>Father |
| 36. Swinney, Helen | 65 | Mickey Touchette<br>Marvin Swinney | Grandmother<br>Mother |
| 37. Swinney, Tim | 39 | Mickey Touchette<br>Marvin Swinney | Uncle<br>Brother |
| 38. Berry, Diana | 7 | Carnella Truss (San Francisco) | Daughter |
| 39. Griffith, Marrian | 15 | Carnella Truss | Sister |
| 40. Griffith, Emmett Jr. | 20 | Carnella Truss | Brother |
| 41. Griffith, Amonda | 17 | Carnella Truss | Sister |
| 42. Kice, Thomas D. | 43 | Wayne Pietila (Petaluma) | Step-father |
| 43. Kice, Thomas D., II | 12 | Wayne Pietila | Half-brother |
| 44. Chaikin, Eugene | 46 | Raphael Chaikin (Newport Beach) | Brother |

HUMAN RIGHTS ABUSES BY JIM JONES (CONTINUED)

| Name of Relative at Jonestown | Age | Petitioners to Forbes Burnham and Cyrus Vance | Relationship to Petitioner |
|---|---|---|---|
| 45. Chaikin, Phyllis | 40 | Raphael Chaikin | Sister-in-law |
| 46. Chaikin, Gail | 16 | Raphael Chaikin | Niece |
| 47. Chaikin, David | 13 | Raphael Chaikin | Nephew |
| 48. Farrell, Barbara L. | 44 | Lena May Pietila (Petaluma)<br>Elwood Leo Holt (Fairfield) | Mother<br>Sister |
| 49. Flowers, Rebecca Ann | 24 | Lena May Pietila<br>Elwood Leo Holt | Sister<br>Niece |
| 50. Tupper, Larry, Jr. | 10 | Laurence Tupper (Chico) | Son |
| 51. Tupper, Ruth | 21 | Laurence Tupper | Daughter |
| 52. Tupper, Mary | 17 | Laurence Tupper | Daughter |
| 53. Tupper, Tim (Jones) | 20 | Laurence Tupper | Son |
| 54. Tupper, Janet | 14 | Laurence Tupper | Daughter |
| 55. Bates, Christine | 73 | Henry W. Haynes (Los Angeles)<br>Mrs. Henry Haynes (Los Angeles) | Sister<br>Sister-in-law |
| 56. Parks, Jerry | 44 | Dennis H. Parks (Ukiah) | Brother |
| 57. Parks, Patricia | 42 | Dennis H. Parks | Sister-in-law |
| 58. Parks, Dale | 27 | Dennis H. Parks | Nephew |
| 59. Parks, Brenda | 17 | Dennis H. Parks | Niece |
| 60. Parks, Tracy | 11 | Dennis H. Parks | Niece |
| 61. Lacy, Georgia | 68 | Phillip Lacy (San Luis Obispo)<br>Frank Lacy (San Francisco) | Mother<br>Wife |
| 62. Briggs, Donna | 15 | Phillip Lacy | Half-sister |
| 63. Liton, Tony | 13 | Phillip Lacy | Half-brother |
| 64. Edwards, James | 58 | Queen Settles (Richmond)<br>Ophelia Robinson (Oakland)<br>Wilhelmina Johnson (Berkeley)<br>Elnora James (Berkeley)<br>Calvin Johnson (San Francisco)<br>Mary Evans (Berkeley) | Uncle<br>Brother<br>Uncle<br>Uncle<br>Uncle<br>Brother |
| 65. Edwards, Irene | 56 | Modenia Belton (Concord)<br>Mildred Womack (Daly City)<br>Edna Smith (San Francisco) | Sister<br>Sister<br>Sister |
| 66. Ponts, Lois | 51 | Cynthia Beam | Mother |

HUMAN RIGHTS ABUSES BY JIM JONES (CONTINUED)

| Name of Relative at Jonestown | Age | Petitioners to Forbes Burnham and Cyrus Vance | Relationship to Petitioner |
|---|---|---|---|
| 67. Parks, Joyce | 32 | Jack Arnold Beam (Ventura) | Sister |
| 68. Beam, Eleanor | 17 | Jack Arnold Beam | Sister |
| 69. Beam, Rheaviana | 53 | Jack Arnold Beam | Mother |
| 70. Beam, Jack | 53 | Jack Arnold Beam | Father |
| 71. Breidenbach, Rocky | 45 | Sam Breidenbach (Fremont) | Mother |
| 72. Breidenbach, Wesley | 19 | Sam Breidenbach | Brother |
| 73. Breidenbach, Melanie | 18 | San Breidenbach | Sister |
| 74. Sneed, Eloise | 70 | Mabel Medlock (Los Angeles) Wade Medlock (Los Angeles) | Sister Sister-in-law |
| 75. Williams, Syola | 66 | Wade & Mabel Medlock | (Same) |
| 76. Johnson, Clara | 46 | Mabel Medlock | Niece |
| 77. Johnson, Tommy | 22 | Mabel Medlock | Nephew |
| 78. Johnson, JoAnn | 19 | Mabel Medlock | Niece |
| 79. Johnson, Joyce | 16 | Mabel Medlock | Niece |
| 80. Johnson, Janice | 17 | Mabel Medlock | Niece |
| 81. King, Charlotte | 80 | Mattye M. Durham (Los Angeles) | Mother |
| 82. Duncan, Regina | 14 | Katie Williams (San Francisco) | Niece |

TOTALS:  82 Relatives in Jonestown   (As of May 10, 1978)
         57 Petitioners

CHILDREN BEING HELD IN JONESTOWN BY JONES IN VIOLATION OF COURT ORDERS:

| Name | Age | Date of California Superior Court order |
|---|---|---|
| 1. Wagner, Mark | 16 | September 29, 1977 |
| 2. Ponts, Donna | 15 | January 6, 1977 |
| 3. Stoen, John Victor | 6 | November 18, 1977 |

# PEOPLE'S TEMPLE—PEOPLE'S TOMB

ACCUSATION OF HUMAN RIGHTS VIOLATIONS BY REV.
JAMES WARREN JONES AGAINST OUR CHILDREN AND
RELATIVES AT THE PEOPLES TEMPLE JUNGLE ENCAMP-
MENT IN GUYANA, SOUTH AMERICA

TO: REV. JAMES WARREN JONES

From: Parents and relatives of children and adults under your
control at "Jonestown", Northwest District, Cooperative
Republic of Guyana

Date: April 11, 1978

## I. INTRODUCTION

We, the undersigned, are the grief-stricken parents and
relatives of the hereinafter-designated persons you arranged
to be transported to Guyana, South America, at a jungle encampment you call "Jonestown". We are advised there are no tele-
phones or exit roads from Jonestown, and that you now have more
than 1,000 U.S. citizens living with you there.

We have allowed nine months to pass since you left the
United States in June 1977. Although certain of us knew it
would do no good to wait before making a group protest, others
of us were willing to wait to see whether you would in fact
respect the fundamental freedoms and dignity of our children
and family members in Jonestown. Sadly, your conduct over the
past year has shown such a flagrant and cruel disregard for
human rights that we have no choice as responsible people but
to make this public accusation and to demand the immediate
elimination of these outrageous abuses.

## II. SUMMARY OF VIOLATIONS

We hereby accuse you, Jim Jones, of the following acts violating the human rights of our family members:

1. Making the following threat calculated to cause alarm for the lives of our relatives: "I can say without hesitation that we are devoted to a decision that it is better even to die than to be constantly harrassed from one continent to the next."

2. Employing physical intimidation and psychological coercion as part of a mind-programming campaign aimed at destroying family ties, discrediting belief in God, and causing contempt for the United States of America.

3. Prohibiting our relatives from leaving Guyana by confiscating their passports and money and by stationing guards around Jonestown to prevent anyone escaping.

4. Depriving them of their right to privacy, free speech, and freedom of association by:

    a. Prohibiting telephone calls;

    b. Prohibiting individual contacts with "outsiders";

    c. Censoring all incoming and outgoing mail;

    d. Extorting silence from relatives in the U.S. by threats to stop all communication;

    e. Preventing our children from seeing us when we travel to Guyana.

The aforesaid conduct by you is a violation of the human rights of our loved ones as guaranteed by Article 55 of the United Nations Charter, and as defined by the Universal Declaration of Human Rights (adopted by the U. N. General Assembly on December 10, 1948). It is also a violation of their constitutional rights as guaranteed by the Constitution of the United States, and as guaranteed by the Constitution of the Cooperative Republic of Guyana (adopted May 26, 1966).

### III. THREAT OF DECISION TO DIE

On March 14, 1978 you, Jim Jones, caused to be written on Peoples Temple stationery a letter "to all U.S. Senators and Members of Congress" complaining of alleged "bureaucratic harrassment" and ending with this chilling threat:

> "[I]t is equally evident that people cannot forever be continually harrassed and beleaguered by such tactics without seeking alternatives that have been presented. I can say without hesitation that we are devoted to a decision that it is better even to die than to be constantly harrassed from one continent to the next."

A copy of your letter is attached as Exhibit A.

We know how exact you are in choosing your words, and there is little doubt that this letter was dictated by you personally since it has been your policy over the years to dictate all letters sent to governmental officials on Temple stationery. Your letter seeks to mask, by the use of irrelevant ideological rhetoric, its real purpose, which is to divert the attention of U.S. Governmental agencies towards your abuses of human rights by putting them on the defensive.

The "1,000 U.S. citizens" you claim to have brought to Guyana include our beloved relatives who are "devoted to a decision that it is better even to die." We frankly do not know if you have become so corrupted by power that you would actually allow a collective "decision" to die, or whether your letter is simply

# PEOPLE'S TEMPLE—PEOPLE'S TOMB

-4-

a bluff designed to deter investigations into your practices.
There is supporting evidence for our concern in the affidavit
of Yolanda Crawford, attached hereto as Exhibit B, which shows
that you have publicly stated in Guyana that you would rather
have your people dead than living in the United States, and
that you have solicited people to lay down their lives for your
cause. You certainly have been successful in making us fearful
as to your intentions.

We hereby give you the opportunity now to publicly repudi-
ate our interpretation of your threat. If you refuse to deny
the apparent meaning of your letter, we demand that you immediately answer the following questions:-

1. When you refer to "a decision that it is better even to
die than to be constantly harrassed", has this "decision" already
been made or is it to be made in the future? If made, when and
where? Were our relatives consulted? Did anybody dissent? By
what moral or legal justification could you possibly make such
a decision on behalf of minor children?

2. When you say you are "devoted" to this decision, does
that mean it is irreversible? If irreversible, at what point will
the alleged "harrassment" have gotten so great as to make death
"better"? Would it be an International Human Rights Commission
investigation, or an on-premises investigation of your operations
by the U. S. Government? Who besides you will decide when that
point "to die" is reached?

We know your psychological coercion of the residents of Jones-
own to be so "totalitarian" that nobody there, including adults,

242

could possibly make such a decision to die freely and voluntarily.
The evidence is that our relatives are in fact hostages, and we
hereby serve notice that should any harm befall them, we will hold
you and Peoples Temple church responsible and will employ every
legal and diplomatic resource to bring you to justice.

IV.  MIND-PROGRAMMING AND INTIMIDATION

The affidavit of Steven A. Katsaris, attached hereto as Exhibit C, is a personal account of his experiences in Guyana.  It
reveals the terrifying effect of your mind-programming on his
daughter, a bright 24-year old, which has caused her to deny belief in God, to renounce family ties, and to manifest symptoms of
sleep-deprivation and a serious personality change.

Yolanda Crawford's affidavit (Exhibit B) is an eye-witness
account of your activities in Guyana by someone present with you.
The affidavit shows that you, Jim Jones, preach there the following doctrines:  a) that you are God and there is no other God,
b) that the United States is the "most evil" nation in the world,
c) that allegiance to your cause must replace family loyalty and
that parents should be handled at a distance for the sole purposes
of collecting inheritances for the cause and of getting them not
to cause trouble.

The evidence also shows that you have instituted the following practices in Guyana:  a) a centralized chain of command whereby
all decisions of significance are to be made by you and once made,
must be followed by Temple members under threat of punishment;
b) the stationing of guards around Jonestown to prevent persons

243

from escaping; and c) the use of degrading punishments (for example, eating hot peppers), sleep-deprivation, food-deprivation, hard labor, and other coercive techniques commonly used in mind-programming.

The evidence also shows that you, Jim Jones, confiscate the passports and monies of people upon their arrival in Guyana, prohibit individual contacts with "outsiders", censor incoming and outgoing mail, prohibit telephone calls by Temple members when in Georgetown, and require Temple members to travel in groups. Ms. Crawford's affidavit also shows that you have publicly threatened that anyone who tries to leave the "cause" will be killed.

The aforesaid conduct by you is a wanton violation of the human rights of our loved ones. It is also a violation of their constitutional rights. The physical intimidation is a violation of the penal codes of the United States and the Cooperative Republic of Guyana.

## V. THE HUMAN RIGHTS BEING VIOLATED

We hereby bring to your attention, Jim Jones, the particular provisions which guarantee human rights and constitutional rights that you are violating:

1. <u>Confiscation of Passports</u>. Your systematic confiscation of passports and all of the monies of Temple members upon their arrival in Guyana is for the purpose of preventing them from leaving and returning to the United States. You are thereby violating Article 13, Section 2 of the Universal Declaration of Human Rights,

# PEOPLE'S TEMPLE—PEOPLE'S TOMB

which reads:

> "Everyone has the right to leave any country, including
> his own, and to return to his country."

Your conduct is also a violation of Article 14 (1) of the Constitution of the Cooperative Republic of Guyana, which reads:

> "No person shall be deprived of his freedom of movement,
> that is to say, the right to move freely throughout
> Guyana,...the right to leave Guyana... ."

2. <u>Prohibiting Telephone Calls</u>. You systematically tell all
Temple members upon their arrival in Georgetown, Guyana that they
are not permitted, under threat of punishment, to make any telephone calls to family members in the United States or elsewhere,
your purpose being to prevent negative information being imparted
to relatives in the U. S. Your additional purpose is to overcome
the bonds of family which might induce a Temple member to wish to
return to his home in the U. S. This conduct is a violation of
Article 19 of the Universal Declaration of Human Rights, which
states:

> "Everyone has the right to freedom of opinion and
> expression; this right includes freedom to hold opin-
> ions without interference and to seek, receive and im-
> part information and ideas through any media and re-
> gardless of frontiers."

This conduct is also a violation of Article 12 (1) of the Guyana
Constitution, which reads:

> "Except with his own consent, no person shall be hin-
> dered in the enjoyment of his freedom of expression,
> that is to say, freedom to hold opinions without inter-
> ference, freedom to communicate ideas and information
> without interference and freedom from interference with
> his correspondance."

# PEOPLE'S TEMPLE—PEOPLE'S TOMB

-8-

3. <u>Prohibiting Contacts With Outsiders</u>.  You systematically require that all Temple members, while in Georgetown, not communicate or visit with "outsiders" and not leave the communal headquarters (41 Lamaha Gardens) unless in association with other Temple members.  You follow the same policy in Jonestown, enforcing your edicts with guards.  Your purpose is to prevent anyone going to the U. S. Embassy and causing them to ask questions how you treat people.  Your additional purpose is to discourage Temple members from being exposed to other religions or philosophies, and from viewing their lives independent of communal obligations. Your conduct is a violation of Article 20, Section 2 of the Universal Declaration of Human Rights, which states:

"No one may be compelled to belong to an association."

It is also a violation of Article 18 of the same Declaration, which states:

"Everyone has the right to freedom of thought, conscience and religion; this right includes freedom to change his religion or belief, and freedom, either alone or in community with others and in public or private, to manifest his religion or belief in teaching, practice, worship and observance."

Your conduct is also a violation of Article 13 (1) of the Guyana Constitution, which reads:

"Except with his own consent, no person shall be hindered in the enjoyment of his freedom of assembly and association, that is to say, his right to assemble freely and associate with other persons."

4. <u>Censoring Mail</u>.  You systematically require that all of the incoming mail and all of the outgoing mail of Temple members be censored by your staff.  Your purpose is to discourage negative

information being "leaked" to people in the U. S. and to prevent facts about the "outside" world reaching Temple members which are at variance with your "party line". This is shown by the affidavit of Ms. Crawford with respect to the Ku Klux Klan marching in the streets. Because mail is the only means of contact available to our loved ones once they are transported to Jonestown, you have thereby effectively cut off all free expression and correspondance. Your conduct is a violation of the right of our relatives to privacy, family, and correspondance under Article 12 of the Universal Declaration of Human Rights, which states:

> "No one shall be subjected to arbitrary interference with his privacy, family, home, or correspondance * * *. Everyone has the right to the protection of the law against such interference."

Your censoring of mail is also a violation of Article 12 (1) of the Guyana Constitution, which is quoted above.

5. Extorting Silence From Relatives. You systematically require that Temple members who write to their family members in the U. S. threaten in their letters that they will stop all further communication if any criticism is made of you or Peoples Temple. For example, Donna Ponts is a 15-year old girl taken to Guyana in July 1977 without her father's knowledge and in violation of a court order requiring her to remain in California unless he gave permission. Attached hereto as Exhibit D is a letter from Donna to her grandmother which starts out saying: "Grandma, Hi! How are you doing? I hope you and everyone else are doing good". It ends as follows:

# PEOPLE'S TEMPLE—PEOPLE'S TOMB

"I am sorry to hear that you called the radio station
but since you did I will not be writing you any more."

Those of us who receive letters from our relatives in Jonestown
find them standardized and unresponsive, as if written by machines.
But since it is all we have, these letters are very precious to us.
You have placed us in the agonizing dilemma of watching helplessly
while the rights of our relatives are violated or losing all contact.  We have chosen, however, not to yield to your extortion,
which is a violation of Article 12 of the Universal Declaration
of Human Rights, quoted above, and of Article 13 (1) of the Guyana
Constitution, also quoted above.

6.  Prohibiting Our Children From Seeing Us.  Five of the
parents who have signed this accusation have travelled from San
Francisco some 5,000 miles in order to see their children since
you took them to Guyana.  The evidence is clear that you have instituted a most pernicious campaign to discredit us in our children's eyes, as can be concluded from the following experiences:

a. Steven A. Katsaris.  On September 26, 1977 Steven A.
Katsaris arrived in Guyana and attempted to meet with his daughter,
Maria.  She was prohibited from meeting with him, duress being employed by you to force her to lie to the U. S. Embassy that she
did not wish to see her father because "he had molested" her.
Mr. Katsaris had with him a letter from Maria inviting him and
saying, "I love you & miss you."  On November 3, 1977 Mr. Katsaris
returned to Guyana to see his daughter, after first obtaining a
promise of assistance from the Guyanese Ambassador to the United

States. After days of waiting, Maria was allowed to see her father but only in the presence of three other Temple members. Maria gave evidence of sleep deprivation and a behavior pattern extremely hostile and different from that ever manifested before. For the details of these two visits, refer to Exhibit C.

b. <u>Howard and Beverly Oliver</u>. On December 19, 1977 Howard and Beverly Oliver, together with their attorney Roger Holmes, arrived in Guyana in order to see their two sons, William S. Oliver (age 17) and Bruce Howard Oliver (age 20). In July 1977 both boys had told their parents they were going to Guyana "for two weeks." The Olivers had a court order from a California Superior Court for the return of William. They also had in their possession letters from each son saying "I love you". After spending eight days without success trying to see their sons, they were told that "Jim Jones had a council meeting" and the decision was that "it was best that we did not see or talk to our sons." Attached as Exhibit E is a handwritten account of Beverly E. Oliver, together with a copy of a letter from each son.

c. <u>Timothy and Grace Stoen</u>. On January 4, 1978 Timothy and Grace Stoen arrived in Guyana in connection with habeas corpus proceedings commenced the preceding August. Although they had a California Superior Court order which ordered you to deliver their six-year old child, John Victor Stoen, to them, you refused to let either parent even see their child. The evidence also shows that you have falsely accused Grace as being "unfit" (see Katsaris affidavit) and that on January 18, 1978 three Temple members surrounded Timothy at Timehri Airport in Guyana and threatened his and Grace's lives if they did not drop legal proceedings (see Crime Report made to Guyana Commissioner of Police Lloyd Barker on January 18, 1978).

The aforesaid conduct on your part constitutes a violation of Article 12 (1) of the Guyana Constitution, quoted above, and Article 12 of the Universal Declaration of Human Rights, which states as follows:

> "No one shall be subjected to arbitrary interference with his...family... ."

## VI. DEMANDS FOR RELIEF

We hereby demand that you, Jim Jones, immediately cease and desist from the aforesaid conduct and that you do the following additional acts immediately:

1. Publicly answer our questions regarding your threat of a collective "decision...to die", and publicly promise U. S. Secretary of State Cyrus Vance and Guyana Prime Minister Forbes Burnham that you will never encourage or solicit the death of any person at Jonestown, whether individually or collectively, for any reason whatsoever;

2. Remove all guards physically preventing our relatives from leaving Jonestown;

3. Return all passports and money taken from our relatives to them for their permanent possession;

4. Permit and encourage our relatives a one-week visit home, at our expense. (Because our relatives have been in Guyana for months (and some, for years) and because it is our belief that they

# PEOPLE'S TEMPLE—PEOPLE'S TOMB

-13-

do not know the full Peoples Temple story and have been preju-
diced against their families, we demand you demonstrate in practice your contention that they are their own agents by permitting
and encouraging our relatives to visit their families in the U. S.
for one week, with our guarantee that we will provide them with
round trip air fare and not interfere with their return at the
end of the family visit should they so choose.)

5. Permit our relatives to write letters to whomever they
wish, uncensored and in private.

6. Permit our relatives to read letters sent to them in private and without censorship.

7. Abide by the orders of the courts in the United States
which you have heretofore ignored.

8. Notify us within three days on your radio-phone network
of your full acceptance and compliance with these demands by contacting:  Steven A. Katsaris, Trinity School, 915 West Church
Street, Ukiah, California 95482; telephone (707) 462-8721.

# PEOPLE'S TEMPLE—PEOPLE'S TOMB

STEVEN A. KATSARIS

AFFIDAVIT

AN ACCOUNT OF SOME OF MY EXPERIENCES WITH PEOPLE'S TEMPLE CHURCH
WHEN I ATTEMPTED TO VISIT MY DAUGHTER IN GUYANA.

In July, 1977 my daughter Maria called me from San Francisco to tell
me she would be going to the People's Temple Agricultural Mission in
Guyana and would be there several weeks. She also informed me that
an article highly prejudicial to People's Temple Church was about to
be published in the New West magazine and asked if I would send a telegram to the publisher in support of the Church's work. I did so stating in the telegram that I believed they were working with people that
our social system had largely neglected. Shortly after the first article appeared in New West magazine my daughter called me from Georgetown to inform me that the article was untrue, politically motivated
and that I should have no concern about her activities in the Church.
She also told me that she wanted to stay several more weeks in Guyana
if that was agreeable with me.

At that time a number of articles appeared in newspapers concerning
the experiences of some members of the Church. I became increasingly
concerned about my daughter when I read that members had been subjected
to various types of psychological and physical coercion. In several
phone calls with my daughter I was assured that she was well and told
her that in several months I would be visiting Washington D.C. on personal business and was considering going on to Guyana afterward to see
her. She appeared enthusiastic and receptive to this idea.

252

My daughter's letters continued to be positive mentioning that she missed me, was concerned about my health, and asked me to send down some mosquito netting and other things that she needed. Early in September 1977 I contacted the Church offices in San Francisco and asked them to inform Maria on their radio phone that I would be arriving in Georgetown on September 26. Several days passed and I received a telephone call from People's Temple Church telling me that radio communication had not been favorable and they were unable to contact my daughter. I told them to keep trying since there still was adequate time before I would be leaving for South America. Several days later at 3:00 in the morning I received a telephone call from an unidentified person who told me that she was part of the group of people who had left People's Temple Church. The purpose of her phone call was to discourage me from going to Guyana. She said it would probably put my daughter in a difficult position. The caller hung up before I could ask any questions. The following night again at approximately 3:00 A.M. I received another phone call. Again the unidentified caller cautioned me about going to Guyana and in more forceful terms told me that it might not be safe for me to do so. The following night I received another telephone call at approximately 4:00 in the morning. This time the caller was a man who told me I should think carefully about my decision to go to Guyana and mentioned that since I lived alone on a ranch in an isolated area my home could be burned down.

The next night on September 14 I received a radio phone call from my daughter Maria. She told me she had learned of my plans to visit her in Guyana and asked that I delay my trip until December when a group

of prominent clergy would be visiting their agricultural project.
The radio phone call was prolonged with many pauses and interruptions
but the essence of the conversation was a series of obstacles presented to me by my daughter to discourage me from visiting. After I told
her that I did not wish to travel with a group of clergy in December
and that I would be going down September 26 she told me that the government of Guyana discouraged visitors due to the "tremendous harrassment" that Jim Jones had been subjected to. She mentioned that he
had been shot at in the jungle. I told my daughter that both she and
Jim Jones knew that I would not harrass them, that I had supported
her membership in the Church and that I would go to the Guyanese Embassy in Washington and ask for clearance to travel to Guyana. After
a pause, Maria told me that it was the policy of the Church not to permit visitors to the project. This seemed extremely strange to me since
I had letters from my daughter indicating that there were daily visitors
to the project. (See attached copy.) I then offered to meet Maria in
Georgetown. She told me she would not be in Guyana but would be in
Venezuela during the time of my intended visit. I suggested meeting
her in Venezuela but she said she could not see me there since she would
only be in that country several days and wanted to spend that time with
her fiance. Her fiance's name reportedly was Larry who was the medical
officer for the agricultural project. I have since learned that another
parent Sherwin Harris has been told that his daughter in Guyana is married to the same doctor. I interpret this ploy as a rather crude attempt to assure parents that their children in the Church are well and
married or about to be married to fine professional people. The radio
phone call was extremely strange and caused me great anxiety because it

did not sound like my daughter was free to speak for herself and certainly her choice of words did not appear natural. The long pauses in the conversation made me suspect she was being coached. When I finally told her that I was upset and frightened and that I would use every legal and diplomatic means to see her she replied that she would not see me even if I did come to Guyana.

The following day I sent a telegram to Rev. Jim Jones telling him of my concern and asking for his reply. (Copy attached.) No reply was ever forthcoming.

Shortly afterwards I left for Washington D.C. where I contacted John Matheny, Military Advisor to Vice President Mondale, and Frank Tuminia of the Guyanese Desk of the State Department. I told them of my concern and solicited their help. I also went to the Guyanese Embassy and was assured that I could travel to Guyana. When I arrived in Georgetown I first went to the United States Embassy and made contact with Mr. Richard McCoy. He showed me a handwritten transcript that was delivered to the Embassy by People's Temple Church member Paula Adams. The message claimed to be from my daughter and had been received in Georgetown via radio phone. It stated that Maria was happy, she was twenty-four years old, engaged to be married and had had a traumatic childhood and did not wish to see her father. Mr. McCoy stated that Paula Adams volunteered background information on me saying that I was a child molester and had sexually abused my daughter and offered that as a reason that Maria did not want to see me. After an unsuccessful attempt to make contact with my daughter in the interior I returned

to Washington D.C. and related my concern to the State Department,
Senator Hubert Humphrey's office, Senator Cranston's office, Congressman Phillip Burton's office, Congressman Lawson's office, the Vice
President's office, and the International Human Rights Commission's
office.

After my return to California I contacted and personally interviewed
as many former members of People's Temple Church as would speak with
me.  To my dismay I learned that my daughter had been received into
the innermost governing body of People's Temple Church and held a position of influence and intimate knowledge of the workings of the movement.  I further learned from former members that she was responsible
for large amounts of money and while in San Francisco would on occasion
have upwards of $200,000.00 in cash and checks in her room at the Tem-
ple.  I ascertained from people who had firsthand knowledge that Maria
had been required to sign an undated suicide note that could be used
to explain her disappearance should she ever attempt to leave the Church
In addition to this she had signed statements incriminating herself
and her family of various imagined bizarre misdeeds.  I was further
told by a former member of the Church that she and Maria had been required to sign statements that the Children's Residential Treatment ,
Center that I direct was involved in a gigantic welfare fraud, that it
was staffed by child molesters and homosexuals, that I myself was a
child molester, and had sexually abused one of the girls in the program
and that the children in our care were being abused.  I was also told
that my daughter's life could be in jeopardy if People's Temple Church
thought that she was about to defect.  In view of the threatening

phone calls that I have received, this appeared to be a definite possibility.  After speaking with Mr. Robert Chilamidos an investigator
for the State of California, with Mr. James Hubert investigator for
the United States Treasury Department, and Mrs. Jan Tespool an investigator for the Mendocino County Sheriff's Department I lived in constant
anxiety for my daughter's safety.  I was convinced that People's Temple
Church was using their humanitarian efforts and social welfare activities to cover for their ultimate goal which is the establishment of
world socialism (facism?) with Jim Jones as their leader and that they
would stop at nothing including calumny, character assassination, blackmail, threats of violence and even murder to achieve their goal.  In
early November I made another trip to Washington D.C. where I convinced
Guyanese Ambassador Lawrence Mann to arrange a meeting between my daughter and me.  He went to Georgetown and while there called me and told
me that Rev. Jones had agreed to the meeting and assured him that he
wanted the members of his Church to have the closest possible relations
with their families.  I was told to come to Georgetown which I did the
following day.  Ambassador Mann met me at my hotel in Georgetown, told
me that Maria would be in the following day and that he had arranged
to take Maria, Mr. McCoy from the United States Embassy and me to dinner
as his guests.  After the dinner he and Mr. McCoy would depart and
Maria and I could have the opportunity to speak privately.  Maria did
not arrive as planned and the Ambassador phoned me explaining that the
Church was having difficulties getting her to Georgetown from the interior.  The following day I was given the same story.  And finally by
Saturday of that week the Ambassador called and told me that Maria would
be arriving at 4:00 p.m.  At 6:00 p.m. that day the Ambassador again

called, appeared somewhat irritated and said he had been informed by the Church's offices in Georgetown that Maria had arrived but was not feeling well and could not go to dinner. I immediately called the Church offices and asked to speak with my daughter. I was told to wait and after a considerable delay was told that Maria was not there and had gone out to dinner. I asked that she call me at my hotel when she returned and was assured that she would. I did not receive a telephone call on Saturday night. However, at 7:15 Sunday morning I was informed by a representative of People's Temple Church that Maria would meet with me in 45 minutes. Ambassador Mann and Mr. McCoy were at the meeting when Maria arrived with four other persons, two men -- one who identified himself as an attorney representing the Church -- an two women. Maria appeared agitated, could not look me in the eye, and did not return my embrace which appeared unusual and even ominous to me. She looked as if she had not slept well or had been deprived of sleep over a long period of time and her general attitude was one of suspicion, hositility and paranoia. She accused me of causing trouble for the Guyanese government and stated that because of my efforts Guyan had been black listed by the International Human Rights Commission. Sh stated further that the Church had been informed by the United States government that I was a member of a conspiracy against the Church and was associated with a right wing congressman who intended to destroy the Church. She accused me of lying to her about my health. When I pointed to Paula Adams, one of the women who accompanied her to the meeting, and asked if she knew that this woman had gone to Mr. McCoy and told him that I had abused my daughter sexually, Maria refused to discuss the subject. When I told her that I had information that she

had signed an undated suicide note, she demanded to know the source
of my information. I told her that was not the important issue and
and that she could alleviate my anxiety by simply telling me it was
not true. She replied that since I would not reveal the source of
my information she would not discuss that subject. In the course
of the conversation with Maria I told her that before leaving for
Guyana I had spoken with Grace Stoen who wanted me to convey her love
and concern to her son John. Maria told me that Grace was an unfit
mother and she had abused her child and that Maria was now the mother
for John. She also told me in a tone that I did not believe possible
from my daughter that if Grace made any attempt to get her child back
she would be sorry. My daughter's affect and the manner in which she
spoke conveyed to me the tone of a serious threat. The entire meeting
was extremely painful for me and depressing. I managed to tell my
daughter that if she ever wanted to return home a ticket would be waiting for her at the Embassy. When I told her of my belief in God and
that somehow things would work out, she and another woman from the
Church were quick to point out to me that they do not believe in God.

After the meeting I went to the airport to catch a flight to New York
City. At the airport I received a message to call Mr. McCoy. In our
telephone conversation he told me that both he and Ambassador Mann
were disturbed by the meeting and believed that something strange was
happening since he could see no reason why the Church should take that
attitude toward me. He told me that he would write to me, but to this
date I have received no communication from him. After arriving in New
York City I proceeded to Washington D.C. where I spent numerous days

contacting as many people in the government as I thought would help me. Most were sympathetic but were quick to point out that since my daughter is 24 years of age and since it appears that she is in Guyana voluntarily there is little they could do to help me.

Since November I have received no communication from Maria and have not attempted to make contact with her since I believe this might be interpreted either as an attempt on my part to get her out of the Church or as a sign that Maria is waivering and is about to defect and might place her life in jeopardy.

*Steven A. Katsaris*

Steven A. Katsaris
Trinity School for Children
Ukiah, California

April 4, 1978

ON _____ April 4 _____ 19 78
before me, the undersigned, a Notary Public in and for said State, personally appeared
--STEVEN A. KATSARIS-- known to me,
to be the person _____ whose name _____ is _____ subscribed to the within instrument,
and acknowledged to me that _____ he _____ executed the same.

WITNESS my hand and official seal.

*Dorothy B. Martin*

Notary Public in and for said State.

CALIFORNIA, MENDOCINO ss.
Y OF

OFFICIAL SEAL
DOROTHY B. MARTIN
NOTARY PUBLIC, CALIFORNIA
PRINCIPAL OFFICE IN
MENDOCINO COUNTY
My Commission Expires January 20, 1981

ACKNOWLEDGMENT—General—Wolcotts Form 233—Rev. 3-64

# PEOPLE'S TEMPLE—PEOPLE'S TOMB

MAILGRAM SERVICE CENTER
MIDDLETOWN, VA . 22645

**western union Mailgram**

2-070073E258002 09/15/77 ICS IPMRNCZ  CSP SROA
1 MGM TDRN UKIAH CA  09-15 0420P EST

STEVEN A  KATSARIS
915 WEST CHURCH ST
UKIAH CA  95482

THIS MAILGRAM IS A  CONFIRMATION COPY  OF THE FOLLOWING MESSAGE:

LT  TDRN UKIAH CA  166  09-15  0204P PDT
INT LT REV JIM JONES PEOPLES TEMPLE AG PROJECT CARE MR MCCOY
US EMBASSY
GEORGETOWN (GUYANA )

RADIOPHONE COMMUNICATIONS SEPTEMBER 14TH WITH DAUGHTER MARIA
KATSARIS CAUSED EXTREME ANXIETY  STOP PLANS TO VISIT HER SEVERAL DAYS
HAVE MET WITH CONFLICTING REASONS WHY SHE CANT SEE HER FATHER STOP I
WAS TOLD THE GUYANA GOVERNMENT DISCOURAGED VISITORS STOP I OFFERED
TO SEEK PERMISSION THROUGH GUYANA EMBASSY  THEN TOLD IT WAS YOUR
POLICY NOT TO PERMIT VISITORS TO PROJECT STOP I OFFERED TO MEET
MARIA IN GEORGETOWN STOP THEN TOLD SHE WOULD BE IN VENEZUELA WITH
BOY FRIEND STOP I SUGGESTED MEET HER IN VENEZUELA STOP THEN TOLD NOT
TO COME TO GUYANA BECAUSE SHE WOULD NOT SEE ME STOP WHAT IS WRONG
CANNOT COMPREHEND DAUGHTERS REFUSAL TO SEE ME STOP AM TRYING HARD TO
BE OBJECTIVE AND NOT BELIEVE IN RECENT PUBLICITY STOP WHY CANT I SEE
MARIA STOP HER RECENT LETTERS INDICATE SHE LOVES AND MISSES HER
FAMILY STOP UPON ASSURANCE BARRY WOOD FORMER DIRECTOR LEGAL SERVE
FOUNDATION MENDOCINO COUNTY I WILL ARRIVE IN GEORGETOWN TO SEE MARIA
SEPTEMBER 26TH AM HURT PUZZLED AND ANXIOUS PLEASE REPLY STEVEN A
KASARIS TRINITY SCHOOL 915 WEST CHURCH STREET UKIAH CALIFORNIA
95482
   STEVEN A KATSARIS

COL 14TH 26TH 915 95482
1625 EST

MGMCOMP MGM

Dear Pop,

How are you feeling? I really hope you are doing better. Has the doctor told you anything else? Please let me know because I am worried about you.

Right now I am in the interior again. I came in by boat which takes about 23 hours. Coming down the Kaituma River is one of my most favorite things. It is hard to describe how beautiful it is. It is so peaceful. I like to sit out on the deck and watch all the scenery. All the animals and birds, plus all the different kinds of tropical plants. The little Amerindian children run out to wave at the boat. The boat is called the Cudjoe — its the one we have at the agricultural project.

I live in a very nice wooden cottage. Some of the cottages here are made out of trulee. It is a kind of plant, sort of like palm leaves, but not really. The Amerindians go out in the bush & cut it down. They dry it out for a few days and then inter-mesh it on a pole frame. It is absolutely waterproof & looks very nice. They are just as durable as the wooden ones.

I do different things around here. I sort of help coordinate, but I also spend time in the medical clinic and in the school. Also I like to go out and work in the fields with the plants. One of the carpenters here is even showing me a few things. I love working with my hands. I can honestly say I have never been happier or healthier. There is something about this climate I guess. Also, being able to work outside without all the tension and pressure of a city. I don't think you realize it until you get away from it.

I know you would love it here since I know how much you like working outside & stuff. Some of the things going here are that you would be interested in are: a huge piggery where are raised pigs. Also there are goats & cattle will be coming in soon. There are also about 10 large chicken houses. I don't know if you have ever heard of the cassava which is a plant grown here. It is kind of like a potatoe. Yours It can be made into bread or fixed like any kind of potatoe. A syrup called casareep which is a popular flavoring in the Caribean can be made from it. It is sort of like soy sauce is to Chinese food. It looks like it only thicker & the taste is not similar. The leafy part is used for animal feed. All these things are processed in a large cassava mill. There are acres & acres of crops. I don't know all of them but some are edocs (also like potato) pineapples, bananas, corn, okra, coffee, breadfruit, different citrus and vegetable. The people here are working on developing new kinds of food. For example there is a large bean called a cutlass bean. They found it has a very high protien content and tryed different ways of using it. Anyway they came up with a way to fix it so it tastes just like sausage patties & even looks like it. Also it can be fixed into a meatloaf only we call it cutlass loaf. It is delicious. It is one of my favorite things & I wouldn't care if I never ate meat again if I had my cutlass patties. That is only one example of the things that have been developed here. The goverment is very impressed and has said this is the best

model of agriculture in the
nation. Some of the other
things that are here are a
saw mill, carpentry shop, school,
medical clinic and other
things which I'll tell you
about next time. I guess
I am really rambling on but
I just want to share my
enthusiasm with you for what
is going on here. I know you
would love it like I said it
is hard to describe all the
beauty of the jungle and all
that is going on at the project too.

Right before I came into
the interior, I helped put together
an exhibit for all the government
officials and the Parliment. It
took a large room and we
had different tables like for
education, agriculture, reacreation,
etc. We also had a long table
where they could sample the
new foods developed at the
project with foods all native
to Guyana. That was a real
big hit. We had papaya fried
pies, plantain chips and bean
burgers (which I also love), a
new kind of breakfast cereal
from plantain & lots of other
stuff. (I think you can tell

... by now I kind of like the food here (Ha Ha) I think I might even get fat if I keep this up!) (there are also anyways back to the exhibit ... (I guess you have figured one reason why I never became a writer is because I don't keep my thoughts organized on paper — I just skip around all over the place) Like I was saying the exhibit — was a big hit and they were very impressed.

Visitors come into the project daily as it has become a sort of model, and is pretty unique. Today 63 teachers & educators came through. They liked the way the school is set up and intend to incorporate some of the same ideas in a school the goverment is opening up nearby.

Yesterday the ambassador to the U.N. came with his wife. They brought a little boy from Venezuela who had suffered from malnutrition — all his brothers & sisters had died from it. He is 4 yrs. old but looks like he is only 2 from being so malnourished. But he is really cute and he is being adopted here at the mission. We have

many children from the local
area living here... One thing
that has been done by the
medical clinic is that gastroento-
nitis (if that's how you spell it —
which I'm sure it's not) has been
virtually wiped out in this area.
_____ Anyway I better stop for
now — I don't want you to
have to read through a whole
lot. But I do have a lot to
tell you! Some feature attractions
from upcoming letters include
✱ more about what I do, ✱ the
school. ✱ the bush, ✱ the animals
here, and much more. Oh! How
could I forget to tell you! — I
am now the proud mother of
3 baby armadillos! There nest
was disturbed out in the
fields which meant the mother
would probably reject them. So
now I am feeding them with
an eye dropper. I hope they make
it. It would be neat to have
little armadillos running around!
_____ One last thing — please,
please, please do not get disturbed by the bad publicity
the church has gotten. I am
more convinced than ever of
conspiratorial & political set-ups.
It is absolutely incredible how
the press can print such a

filthy bunch of lies and are allowed to get by with it. They refuse to print what we have had to say or to show the truth. I guess the other makes for more sensational reading. I am not suprised though. A society that is based on economic inequality and classism is certainly not going to let and organization advocating economic & racial equality exist too easily. But no matter what they think, they will not suceed. This group has done too much good and helped to many people. What is unfortunate is that the mentality of many people is un-objective when it comes to the media. Most people believe everything they hear on the news and read in the papers. Even mom said to me, "Well they wouldn't print it if it wasn't true." I love her very much & I think she is very intelligent but that is how she sees it too. I you happen to talk to her please tell her not to worry about it since there isn't a thing to even be worried about in the first place. What I worry about + resent is that such a thing has been allowed to happen. What is ironic is that we have always been the first to stand for freedom of the press + 5th amendment rights. I can certainly tell you I will have a hard time believing the papers anymore. At least I will look at what is being said with a very scrutinizing eye. Well that's also enough of that! If you want to know anything just ask me. The fools would be rather hard pressed to look around this place which is just one aspect of our work — and continue with what they are saying — when hundreds of needy people are being clothed, housed + fed + given good medical care.

I am also writing Mom + if you send me Tanya's address I will write her too. The mail will probably take about 2 wks to get to me in the interior — so hurry up + write! One of these times I will get some guy in the U.S. to set up a phone patch + will call you on the radio! Bye for now. I love you + miss you. So write. Your daughter, Maria

P.S. THIS IS REALLY MY WRITING !!!

April – 197.
S. F. C.

in July – 1977 my sons told me
they wanted to go to Guyana, for two
weeks. They had been several places,
with the church members, & prior force,
so we agreed for them to go.

On July 26, 1977 we my husband,
and I left for work, leaving both sons
at home in bed sleep. When we got
home, we did not know they had left
for Guyana, No one even told or called
us. We did talk to them by People Temple
radio, Two or three time.

About three weeks after they had
left my husband & I went to the church
(People Temple) & talked to Marceline Jones,
in the present of Leona Collier & Harriett Tropp,
We asked for the return of our sons, They all
got angry, but Marceline said she would
call Jim & tell him. But neither boy came
home & no more was mention.

The same week I call to People
Temple Church & talked to Jane Mueshman I
told her I wanted to talk to my sons on
the hamon's radio She told me I would

have to talk to Charles Gary, I called him
he told me there would not be no
communication with my sons at all.

On. Nov-28-77 We went to Court
for the return of William Oliver at that time
he was still a minor age 17 yrs. The
Court ruled that Jim Jones had to send him
home. (S.4.) Charles Gary said that we
would have to send for William because Jim
Jones was not going to pay his fare back.
That same day We sent a ticket to Pan American
in Guyana in William Oliver named, the ticket
was unused.

On Dec -19-77 Mr. Rozger Holmes
Our attorney Mr. Olive & myself, went to
Guyana. Jim Jones had a council meeting
and there descion for it was best that
We did not see or talk to our sons, that
is what we was told by the Guyanese Prime
Minister of Foreign Affend. Mr. Fred Wells

We stayed 8 -days but Jones
said no. at this point we do not know
if our sons is dead or alived. for we have
not heard from them since Aug -1977.
_____
Beverly E. Oliver

271

Dear Mom & Dad

How is everything going? Everything with me is going just fine. I'm here in Jonestown and all I got to say is that you have to see it to believe it, it's the most beautiful place I've ever seen. It's called Jonestown because that what it is a small town. I spend half the morning working in the mill where they make bread the rest of the day trucking wood watching and/or going swimming or what ever. This is the place I would want to spend the rest of my life so as of now I'm staying. I love you both and think of the both of you everyday. (not just mom but you too dad). I often think of the things you taught me about being a man, you were right since I been here I feel like I'm grown alot. I really appreciate the time you took with me even tho alot of the times I would get mad and walk away. Thank for everything. (and I really mean it). If I didn't have the *love* you both gave to me as *good* parents my life would be rough, but instead its *so* sweet. The people are all nice and friendly. The only thing that would make it better is if you were here to *see* The beauty which I'm now seeing now. <u>Please write *soon* and stay in contact.</u>

Love you always

Bruce Olivir

Dear Mom & Dad.

How are you doing? Fine I hope...
I'm doing fine here,it's very
very beutiful here.. The wheather
nice & the people here are very.
friendly,Always willing to help you.
The only sorrow I have is that
you guys are not here with me..
Also make sure you tell Gramma
I love every very much.And miss
her her to. Mom I hope you will come
here soon and share all the
happiness I have with me. Once
you're here all pressure & tension
Leaves. Tell Dad I wish him all
the success in his business and I
often find my self thinking about
him. Well I have to go now
I'll be writing again real
soon.

Love ya

P.S Mom tell Evonne I missed
her to. And Work hard Its Worth
it.
Your son Bill
Oliver

SIGNATURES OF PETITIONERS FOR ELIMINATION OF HUMAN RIGHTS

VIOLATIONS IN GUYANA BY REV. JAMES JONES

| Name of Relative at Jonestown, Guyana | Age | Signature of Petitioner | Relation |
|---|---|---|---|
| Ellen Louise Kerns (Sibis) | 55 | Ruth Reinhardt | mother |
| Carol Ann Kerns | 19 | Ruth Reinhardt | sister |
| Magnolia Harris | 61 | Sylvia White | mother |
| Magnolia Harris | | Reinada White | grandmother |
| Liane Harris | 21 | Steven Harris | Father |
| MARCIA SIMON | 22 | Leon Simon | Daughter |
| BARBARA SIMON | 22 | Leon Simon | Daughter |
| Liane Harris | 21 | Liz Harris | sister |
| Bruce Oliver | 20 | | |
| William Oliver | 18 | Gerald Oliver | Father |
| Donna Fitz | | Gerald White | Father |
| Judy Lynn Houston | 13 | Nadyne L. Houston | Granddaughter |
| Patricia Ann Houston | 14 | Nadyne L. Houston | Granddaughter |
| Judy Houston | 13 | | Aunt |
| Patricia Houston | 14 | | Aunt |
| Judy Houston | 13 | Robert H. Houston | Grandfather |
| Patricia Houston | 14 | Robert H. Houston | Grandfather |
| Bruce Oliver | 20 | Beverly Oliver | Mother |
| William Oliver | 15 | | |
| John Victor Stoen | 6 | Timothy O. Stoen | Father |
| Mike Rozynko | 20 | | Sister |
| | | | Brother-in-law |
| Chris Rozynko | 22 | | Sister |
| | | | Brother-in-law |

# PEOPLE'S TEMPLE—PEOPLE'S TOMB

| Name of Relative at Jonestown, Guyana | Age | Signature of Petitioner | Relationship |
|---|---|---|---|
| 1. Charles Touchette | 41 | Micky Touchette | father |
| 2. Joyce Touchette | 45 | Micky Touchette | mother |
| 3. Mike Touchette | 25 | Micky Touchette | brother |
| 4. Al Touchette | 23 | Micky Touchette | brother |
| 5. Michelle Touchette | 19 | Micky Touchette | sister |
| 6. Cleve Swinney | 60+ | Micky Touchette | grandfather |
| 7. Helen Swinney | 60+ | Micky Touchette | grandmother |
| 8. Tim Swinney | 30+ | Mickey Touchette | uncle |
| 9. Mary Griffith | 52 | Louise Blanchard | sister |
| 10. Mariam Griffith | 14 | Louise Blanchard | aunt |
| 11. Ormond Griffith | 17 | Louise Blanchard | aunt |
| 12. Emmith Griffith | 19 | Louise Blanchard | |
| 13. Mary Lee Griffith | 52 | Rose Davis | aunt |
| 14. Amanda Griffith | 17 | Rose Davis | cousin |
| 15. Emmit Griffith Jr. | 19 | Rose Davis | cousin |
| 16. Mariam Griffith | 15 | Rose Davis | cousin |
| 17. Daena Berry | 7 | Rose Davis | cousin |
| 18. Cornellia Sykes Jr. | 14 | Rose Davis | cousin |
| 19. John Victor Stoen | 6 | Grace L. Stoen | son |
| 20. Maria S. Katsaris | 24 | Steven A. Katsaris | daughter |
| 21. Mark Andrew Sly | 17 | Neva Jean Sly | son |
| 22. Donald E. Sly | 42 | Neva Jean Sly | husband |

276

# PEOPLE'S TEMPLE—PEOPLE'S TOMB

| | Name of Relative at Jonestown, Guyana | Age | Signature of Petitioner | Relationship |
|---|---|---|---|---|
| 1. | Charles Touchette | 47 | Mickey Touchette | father |
| 2. | Joyce Touchette | 45 | Mickey Touchette | Mother |
| 3. | Mike Touchette | 25 | Mickey Touchett | Brother |
| 4. | Al Touchette | 23 | Mickey Touchette | Brother |
| 5. | Michelle Touchette | 19 | Mickey Touchette | Sister |
| 6. | Cleve Swinney | 60 | Mickey Touchette | Grandfather |
| 7. | Helen Swinney | 60 | Mickey Touchette | Grandmother |
| 8. | Tim Swinney | 30's late | Mickey Touchette | Uncle |
| 9. | Mary Griffith | 52 | Louise Blanchard | Sister |
| 10. | Marrien Griffith | | Louise Blanchard | aunt |
| 11. | Amonda Griffith | | Louise Blanchard | aunt |
| 12. | Emmith Griffith | | Louise Blanchard | aunt |
| 13. | Mary Griffith | 52 | Rose Davis | aunt |
| 14. | Warrien Griffith | 14 | Rose Davis | cousin |
| 15. | Amonda Griffith | 17 | Rose Davis | cousin |
| 16. | Emmith Griffith | 19 | Rose Davis | cousin |
| 17. | Daina Berry | 7 | Rose Davis | cousin |
| 18. | Cornellia Duesa | 14 | Rose Davis | cousin |
| 19. | Emmith Griffith | | Cornellia Tress | father |
| 20. | Mary Griffith | | Cornellia Tress | mother |
| 21. | Emmith Griffith Jr | | Cornellia Tress | brother |
| 22. | Amonda Griffith | | Cornellia Tress | sister |
| 23. | Warren Griffith | | Cornellia Tress | brother |
| 24. | Daina Griffith | | Cornellia Tress | sister |
| 25. | John Victor Dew | 6 | Rose F. Dew | son |

# PEOPLE'S TEMPLE—PEOPLE'S TOMB

SIGNATURES OF PETITIONERS FOR ELIMINATION OF HUMAN RIGHTS
VIOLATIONS IN GUYANA BY REV. JAMES JONES

| Name of Relative at Jonestown, Guyana | Age | Signature of Petitioner | Relation |
|---|---|---|---|
| Mark Wagner | 16 | Richard Wagner | father |
| | | Richard Wagner | father |
| | | Carol Boyd | aunt |
| | | Carol Boyd | aunt |
| | | Robert H. Houston | Grandinglse |
| | | Robert H. Houston | grandinglse |
| | | Madgre L. Houston | Granddaughter |
| | | Madge L. Houston | Granddaughter |
| | | Ronald White | father |
| | | Henri Oliver | Father |
| Pierre Oliver | 19 | | |
| William Oliver | 15 | | |
| Liane Harris | 21 | Liz Harris | sister |
| MARIIA SIMON | 22 | Leon Simon | |
| BARBARA SIMON | 22 | Leon Simon | FATHER |
| Liane Harris | 21 | Bruce Harris | Father |
| Mark Andrew Sly | 17 | Nana Jean Sly | Son |
| Donald E. Sly | 42 | Nana Jean Sly | Husband |
| Ellen L. Kerns (Selmes) | 55 | Ruth Reinhardt | mother |
| Carol Ann Kerns | 19 | Ruth Reinhardt | sister |
| Marquina Harris | 61 | Virginia White | Mother |
| | 61 | | |

278

# APPENDIX B

**Timothy Oliver Stoen**

ATTORNEY AT LAW
120 MONTGOMERY STREET, SUITE 1700
SAN FRANCISCO, CALIFORNIA 94104
TELEPHONE (415) 391-5020

March 16, 1978

Ross E. Case
285 Carleton Drive
Ukiah, California 95482

Re:  Trinidad Insurance companies

Dear Ross:

Thank you for sending me the photocopies of the yellow
pages of the Trinidad & Tobago telephone company per-
taining to insurance companies.

I have reviewed each company but am unable to remember
which particular one is handling the Jonestown account.

I hope you are well and happy.  Please give my warm
regards to my friends in Ukiah.  I will come up for one
of your Thursday evening meetings as soon as my schedule
allows.  Right now I am extremely busy fighting to get
back my son.  I will let you know when I can come.

Kindest personal regards.

Sincerely,

*Timothy*

Timothy Oliver Stoen

# PEOPLE'S TEMPLE—PEOPLE'S TOMB

**16976**

Recording requested by:
People's Temple of the Disciples
of Christ, a Non-profit Corporation

RECORDED AT REQUEST OF

*Thomas Kice*

воок **764** PAGE **46**

MAY 6 11 59 AM '68

When recorded mail to:
Financial Secretary
People's Temple of the Disciples
of Christ
P. O. Box 214
Redwood Valley, California 95470

OFFICIAL RECORDS
MENDOCINO COUNTY, CALIF.
*Dilo Richardson*
RECORDER

$ 2 80

No Tax Due

Mail tax statements to the
return address above

Affix IRS $ _____

## QUITCLAIM DEED

THOMAS DAVID KICE and WANDA FAYE KICE, husband and wife, do
remise, release and quitclaim to People's Temple of the Disciples of
Christ, a non-profit corporation, their right, title and interest in
the property in the County of Mendocino, State of California,
described as:

BEGINNING at the Northwest corner of that parcel of land conveyed to
C.A. Jenkins et ux, by deed recorded May 17, 1954 in Book 370 of
Official Records, page 454, Mendocino County Records, said Northwest
corner being on the Easterly line of the County Road in the Northeast
quarter of the Southeast quarter of Section 7, Township 17 North, Range
12 West, Mount Diablo Meridian; thence from said point of beginning
Northerly along the Easterly line of said County Road a distance of 208
feet to the Southerly line of that parcel of land conveyed to Frank M.
Dunnebeck and wife by deed recorded January 16, 1958 in Book 476 of
Official Records, at page 332, Mendocino County Records; thence Easterly
along said Southerly line a distance of 1050 feet to an angle point in
said Southerly line; thence South along said Southerly line a distance
of 208 feet, more or less, to the North line of C.A.Jenkins as first
above mentioned; thence Westerly along the North line of said C.A.Jenkins,
a distance of 1050 feet, more or less to the point of beginning. Being
a portion of the Northeast quarter of the Southeast quarter of Section
7 and of Lot 12 of Section 8, Township 17 North, Range 12 West, Mount
Diablo Meridian, according to the official plat of the survey of said
land on file in the Bureau of Land Management,approved June 17,1879.

TOGETHER with all the right of the grantors as set forth in that Grant
of Easement executed by Frank S. Dunnebeck, et al on the 21st day of
November, 1966,recorded on the 23rd day of November, 1966, in Liber
729at page 200 Official Records of Mendocino County, California, and
TOGETHER with an easement for the purpose of ingress and egress over the
presently existing road on the lands of Grantors as described in that
certain Deed of Trust executed by Grantors and recorded in Vol.459,
Official Records, at page 93, Mendocino County Records.

Dated: May 6, 1968.     *Thomas David Kice*
                        Thomas David Kice

Dated: May 6, 1968.     *Wanda Faye Kice*
                        Wanda Faye Kice

воок **764** PAGE **46**

# PEOPLE'S TEMPLE—PEOPLE'S TOMB

MENDOCINO COUNTY
OFFICIAL RECORDS

STATE OF CALIFORNIA )
                    ) ss.
COUNTY OF MENDOCINO )

On May 6, 1968, before me, the undersigned
Notary Public, personally appeared Thomas David Kice and
Wanda Faye Kice, known to me to be the persons whose names
are subscribed to this instrument and acknowledged that
they executed it.

_Timothy O. Stoen_
Timothy O. Stoen
Notary Public for the State of California

[S E A L]

OFFICIAL SEAL
TIMOTHY O. STOEN
NOTARY PUBLIC, CALIFORNIA
PRINCIPAL OFFICE IN
MENDOCINO COUNTY
My Commission Expires March 26, 1972

-2-

A TRANSFER OF DEEDS OF PROPERTY TO PEOPLES TEMPLE OF
DISCIPLES OF CHRIST

SOURCE: GENERAL INDEX: GRANTEES, N-R, FROM JAN. 1, 1967, Mendocino Cty, CA

| Date | NAME | BOOK | PAGE |
|------|------|------|------|
| May 6, 1968 | Thomas David Kice | 764 | 46 |
| June 17, 1968 | James Jones | 767 | 170 |
| Oct. 7, 1969 | Virgil J. Clark | 801 | 643 |
| Mar. 5, 1969 | Marvin D. Ford | 811 | 734 |
| Sept. 1, 1970 | Lucille V. Furlong | 825 | 739 |
| Sept. 1, 1970 | Lucille V. Furlong | 825 | 741 |
| Sept 29, 1971 | Carson B. Robenalt | 863 | 393 |
| Dec. 31, 1971 | Russell Bland Strickland | 872 | 215 |

GENERAL INDEX: GRANTEES, N-R, FROM JAN. 1, 1972, Mendocino County, Calif.

| Date | NAME | BOOK | PAGE |
|------|------|------|------|
| Jan. 5, 1972 | Ernest R. Cassells | 872 | 557 |
| Apr. 6, 1972 | Timothy O. Stoen | 883 | 537 |
| Sept. 1, 1972 | Joe D. Slater | 893 | 634 |
| Jan. 16, 1973 | Robert Newhall | 912 | 130 |
| Feb. 8, 1973 | Eugene Chaikin | 914 | 590 |
| Feb. 8, 1973 | Linda Amos | 914 | 592 |
| Feb. 8, 1973 | James R. Purifoy | 914 | 594 |
| Feb. 9, 1973 | Charles F. Cliburn | 914 | 567 |
| June 6, 1973 | Phyllis Chaikin | 927 | 445 |
| Jan. 2, 1974 | Janet T. Phillips (By Atty-in Fact) | 949 | 216 |
| Aug. 12, 1974 | Archie J. Ijames | 972 | 444 |
| Jan. 24, 1975 | Russell B. Strickland (Cross-defendant) | 988 | 424 |
| | Judg quieting Title & Estab Rights of Way | | |
| Feb. 13, 1975 | Russell B. Strickland (Cross-defendant) | 990 | 34 |
| | Judg quieting Title & Estab Rights of Way | | |
| July 11, 1975 | Albert D. Spencer | 1006 | 219 |
| Sept. 22, 1975 | Marvin D. Swinney | 1013 | 673 |

GENERAL INDEX: GRANTEES, L-R, FROM JAN. 1, 1976, Mendocino County, Calif.

| Date | NAME | BOOK | PAGE |
|------|------|------|------|
| Mar. 16, 1976 | Hyacinth Catherine Thrash | 1032 | 681 |
| May 7, 1976 | Danny Kutulas | 1039 | 321 |
| May 7, 1976 | Emma Jane Jurado | 1039 | 373 |
| July 9, 1976 | Raymond Godshalk | 1047 | 19 |
| July 9, 1976 | Leo James Bertolonci | 1047 | 23-24 |
| Aug. 22, 1976 | James R. Purifoy | 1052 | 708 |
| Aug. 30, 1976 | Grace L. Stoen | 1053 | 736-739 |
| Sept. 16, 1976 | Eugene B. Chaikin | 1056 | 173 |
| Sept. 16, 1976 | Claud B. Love, Jr. | 1056 | 185 |
| Sept. 16, 1976 | Claud B. Love, Jr. | 1056 | 198 |

# PEOPLE'S TEMPLE—PEOPLE'S TOMB

1. Chief Medical Officer of the Ministry of Health, Guyana: "Impressive."

2. Charge D'Affaires, new assistant to U.N. Ambassador Andrew Young: "I am impressed."

3. Officer in Charge of Guyana, Jamaica, and Trinidad & Tobago, U.S. Department of State: "Impressive work."

4. Minister of Foreign Affairs, Guyana: "Peace and love in action."

5. Minister of Education, Guyana: "Very impressive."

6. Regional Development Officer, North West Region, Guyana: "Very progressive."

7. Chief Official in the Ministry of Education, Guyana: "Very much impressed with everything, thanks."

8. Head Dental Instructor, University of Guyana: "Excellent community project."

9. British High Commissioner in Guyana: "A most impressive start and I wish you all success."

10. Chancellor of the University of Guyana: "Impressive."

11. Minister of Agriculture, Guyana: "Very interesting, keep it up."

12. Minister of Works and Transportation, Guyana: "Very impressed with progress since I visited one year ago."

13. Permanent Secretary of Ministry of Works and Transportation: "A wonderful experience, a model village community to be emulated."

14. Assistant Director General of National Service of Guyana: "Excellent."

15. United States Consulate in Guyana: "A very pleasant day in a very pleasant atmosphere."

16. A writer from one of the largest news agencies in the world: "It's very, very impressive. Thank you for this opportunity and best wishes."

17. Regional Minister, North West Region, Guyana: "Keep up the good work."

18. Thirty-five teachers from the McKenzie District: "Fantastic, beyond one's imagination, miraculous, beautiful, a true example of socialist living." "Amazing, impressive."

19. Head and one of the original founders of the Marco Medical Net: "Incredible, fantastic."

# PEOPLE'S TEMPLE—PEOPLE'S TOMB

P.O. Box 15023

San Francisco, CA 94115

The "Concerned Relatives" is an elaborate hoax. The Charges about
our organization's community are all vicious lies and part of a
right-wing McCarthy-like attack on Rev. Jim Jones and our
congregation. We are here to expose what Tim Stoen, the main
organizer and ringleader of these efforts, is really up to. He
has been in contact with an aerial reconnaissance outfit and is
secretly plotting with others in the group to actually land
mercenaries on the project. We have definite evidence in hand and
are investigating this further.

Another member of this group who is supposedly so "concerned" about
"Human rights" actually told us only yesterday that Tim Stoen could
"drop things on the project and he might even be planning to do it".

The groups that is assembled here is staging this pseudo-event to
cover up these outrageous plans to violate laws and commit criminal
acts against innocent people. The high-sounding complaints about
human rights violations are a subterfuge. If anyone is violating
human rights, it is Tim Stoen and his lunatic outfit. The
people called "Concerned Relatives" have actually tried to cut
off our only outside source of medical assistance that has been
life-saving.

Hundreds of people with relatives in Guyana maintain regular
contact and are free to come and visit. And many have done so.
In fact relatives who are not Residents of the community are free
to come and go and a guest house is being built to accomodate
visitors. Literally hundreds of visitors have come and been
highly complimentary of what is being accomplished. For a long

time we have been trying to explain that what the public is seeing is a deliberate front for a politically-motivated conspiracy to destroy the organization and Rev. Jones. They have attempted to bribe and coerce people and to denounce Rev. Jones; they have attempted to cut off senior members' old age pensions and Social Security; to ransack shipments of vital supplies; and now plan to send in mercenaries. These are just a few highlights of what is behind the smokescreen of lies and pious pronouncements of this conspiracy led by Mr. Stoen.

Recent visitors to the project have called it a utopia. The statement of a doctor who heads a medical network of nearly a thousand doctors was: "It's mind-boggling to see how you have carved out of the jungle a community that looks just like one in the U.S. and with all the public utilities". When the Foreign Minister of Guyana visited the project he called it a stunning example of cooperation and love. The Chairman of the Guyana Livestock Corporation, a veterinarian who has traveled and studied in many countries, said: "The community is the purest form of cooperative living I have ever seen". Dr. De Costa, a dentist from India, who founded a dental school which he heads in Guyana, said the health care is fantastic. As an example, he said he found only two cavities after examining eighty children. He said that is unheard of.

As many as 30 visitors, guests from Guyana and from around the world, visit the community everyday. All are impressed. The comment of one government Minister sums up the feelings of many: "A model village community to be emulated the world over".

# CERTIFICATE OF DEATH

## STATE OF CALIFORNIA—DEPARTMENT OF PUBLIC HEALTH

2300-308

| | | |
|---|---|---|
| 1A NAME OF DECEASED—FIRST NAME | 1B MIDDLE NAME | 1C LAST NAME |
| TRUTH | NONE | HART |
| 2 LOCAL REGISTERED DISTRICT AND CERTIFICATE NUMBER | | |
| 3 SEX | 4 COLOR OR RACE | 5 BIRTHPLACE STATE OR FOREIGN COUNTRY |
| FEMALE | NEGRO | PENNSYLVANIA |
| 6 DATE OF BIRTH | 7 AGE IF UNDER ONE YEAR | |
| Dec. 9, 1907 | 66 YEARS | |
| DATE OF DEATH—MONTH DAY YEAR | HOUR |
| JULY 16, 1974 | 11:00 A. |
| 8 NAME AND BIRTHPLACE OF FATHER | 9 MAIDEN NAME AND BIRTHPLACE OF MOTHER |
| UK. | UK. |
| 10 CITIZEN OF WHAT COUNTRY | 11 SOCIAL SECURITY NUMBER |
| U.S.A. | 203 14 0318 |
| 12 NAME OF SURVIVING SPOUSE (IF WIFE ENTER MAIDEN NAME) |
| 12a WAS DECEASED EVER IN U.S. ARMED FORCES | |
| 13 NAME OF SURVIVING SPOUSE | |
| 14 LAST OCCUPATION | 15 | 16 NAME OF LAST EMPLOYING COMPANY OR FIRM |
| UK. | | |
| 17 KIND OF INDUSTRY OR BUSINESS | |

### PLACE OF DEATH

| | | |
|---|---|---|
| 18A PLACE OF DEATH—NAME OF HOSPITAL OR OTHER IN-PATIENT FACILITY | 18B STREET ADDRESS—STREET AND NUMBER OR LOCATION | |
| Maribelle Rest Home | 410 Mary St. | |
| 18C CITY OR TOWN | 18B COUNTY | |
| Ukiah | Mendocino | |

### USUAL RESIDENCE

| | | |
|---|---|---|
| 19A USUAL RESIDENCE—STREET ADDRESS-STREET AND NUMBER OR LOCATION | 19B INSIDE CITY CORPORATE LIMITS | |
| 410 Mary St. | YES | |
| 19C CITY OR TOWN | 19D COUNTY | 19E STATE |
| UK. | MENDOCINO | CALIFORNIA |
| 20 NAME AND MAILING ADDRESS OF INFORMANT | |
| Maribelle Rest Home | |
| 410 Mary St. | |
| Ukiah, Calif. | |

### PHYSICIAN'S OR CORONER'S CERTIFICATION

| | |
|---|---|
| 21 CORONER | |
| INVESTIGATION | |
| 22a DATE | 22b DATE |
| 7-19-74 | 7-19-74 |
| 24 | |

### FUNERAL DIRECTOR AND LOCAL REGISTRAR

| | | |
|---|---|---|
| 22a PLACE OF BURIAL OR ENTOMBMENT | 23 NAME OF CEMETERY OR CREMATORY | |
| BURIAL | UKIAH CEMETERY | |
| 25 NAME OF FUNERAL DIRECTOR OR PERSON ACTING AS SUCH | 26 | 27 LOCAL REGISTRAR |
| EVERSMAN MORTUARY | | |
| 28 DATE RECEIVED | |
| JUL 19 1974 | |

### CAUSE OF DEATH

29 PART I. DEATH WAS CAUSED BY — ENTER ONLY ONE CAUSE PER LINE FOR A, B AND C

| | |
|---|---|
| IMMEDIATE CAUSE (A) | CONGESTIVE HEART FAILURE |
| CONDITIONS IF ANY WHICH GAVE RISE TO THE IMMEDIATE CAUSE (A) STATING THE UNDERLYING CAUSE LAST (B) | RHEUMATIC HEART DISEASE |
| (C) | |

30 PART II. OTHER SIGNIFICANT CONDITIONS—CONTRIBUTING TO DEATH BUT NOT RELATED TO THE IMMEDIATE CAUSE GIVEN IN PART I

288